MARTY SEZ...
VOLUME 2

More Secrets of
Winning Bridge

By Marty Bergen

Bergen Books

Bergen Books
9 River Chase Terrace
Palm Beach Gardens, FL 33418-6817

First Edition published 2002.
Printed in the United States of America.
10 9 8 7 6 5 4 3 2 1

First Printing: August, 2002

Library of Congress Control Number: 2001118235

ISBN 0-9716636-2-9

Dedication

*In Memory of
Jodi Shuman*

*The nicest person
I have ever known.*

Contents

BRIDGE BOOKS BY MARTY BERGEN

Marty Sez

POINTS SCHMOINTS!

More POINTS SCHMOINTS!

Introduction to Negative Doubles

Negative Doubles

Better Bidding with Bergen, Volume I

Better Bidding with Bergen, Volume II

Everyone's Guide to the New Convention Card

ACKNOWLEDGEMENTS

Layout, cover design, and editing by
Hammond Graphics.

My very special thanks to: Cheryl Bergen, Gary
Blaiss, Nancy Deal, Ned Downey, Pete Filandro,
Jim Garnher, Terry Gerber, Meredith Gunter,
Pat Harrington, Steve Jones, Doris Katz, David
Lesko, Patty Magnus, Harriet and Dave Morris,
Phyllis Nicholson, Mary and Richard Oshlag,
Jesse Reisman, Jeff Rubens, Michael
Schneider, Maggie Sparrow, Tom Spector,
Merle Stetser, and Bobby Stinebaugh.

The Official Encyclopedia of Bridge – Fifth Edition by
Alan Truscott, Henry and Dorthy Francis.

STOP – READ THIS

1. **VOB** stands for Enough **V**alues to **O**pen the **B**idding, but not much more.

2. The player with the bidding decision to make is indicated by three question marks: ??? For consistency, South is always that player, and his hand is the one displayed.

3. Every bidding diagram begins with West.

West	North	East	South
—	—	—	2♡
All Pass			

The dashes are place holders, and in the example above, show that the auction did not begin with West, North, or East. The dealer was South. The "—" does not indicate a "Pass."

MARTY SEZ 2 BIDDING STYLE

Opening Bids

Five-card majors in 1st and 2nd seat.
Light opening bids, based on the Rule of 20.
1NT opening bid = 15-17 HCP.
2NT opening bid = 20-21 HCP.
2♣ opening is strong, artificial, and forcing.
Weak two-bids in diamonds, hearts, and spades.
Preempts may be light.

Responding

Limit raises — all suits.
After notrump: Jacoby Transfers and Stayman.

Slam Bidding

Blackwood — traditional, not Roman Key Card.

Competitive

Michaels Cue-Bid, Unusual Notrump.

Chapter 1

Getting Off
on the
Right Foot

YOU TALK TOO MUCH

Bidding can be defined as an exchange of relevant information. You don't have to talk about every suit in your hand.

West's 3♢ bid seemed normal at the time. The next thing he knew, he found himself "in over his head."

West	West	East	East
♠ A K Q J 10 6	1♠	1NT	♠ —
♡ K	3♢	4♢	♡ Q 9 7 6 2
♢ A J 7 6	4♠	5♢	♢ K Q 9 8 4
♣ Q 5	oops!		♣ 6 4 2

West was delighted to jump-shift with his 20 HCP. East was equally delighted to raise to 4♢ with his great support. Obviously, he could hardly pass 4♠.

What went wrong? There was no need for West to introduce diamonds when he always intended to play in spades. Opener should have rebid 4♠ at his second turn, promising a great hand with a self-sufficient suit.

The bottom line: When you know where you want to play, get there ASAP.

IT AIN'T OVER TILL IT'S OVER

When your partner thinks for a long time and then passes, you are NOT barred.

This situation is one of the most misunderstood in all of bridge. Sometimes, a player has a difficult bidding problem. There is absolutely nothing wrong with thinking about what to do. If you don't intend to think, then bridge is not the game for you.

When partner takes extra time, your responsibilities are the same regardless of whether he bids, passes, or doubles. Yes, you noticed the break in tempo; how could you not? Regardless, you must try your best to ignore his hesitation and bid your hand "normally."

Of course, even in the best of circumstances, the question of "what's normal" can vary depending on whom you talk to. Keep in mind — as always, number of HCP is not the key. And if you're concerned that an opponent may have been "unduly influenced," don't say a word, just call the director.

Here are two examples of how to react after a slow pass from your partner.

14

IT AIN'T OVER...CONTINUED

In each case, Pass** indicates a "very slow pass."

West	North	East	South
—	1♠	Pass	2♠
Pass	Pass**	3♦	???

♠ A 6 5   ♡ Q 8 6   ♢ J 6 4   ♣ Q 7 5 2

Pass. Yes, you have more HCP than you might have. However, other than the ♠A, the value of your "soft" honor cards is questionable. Any action now would be taking advantage of partner's hesitation.

West	North	East	South
1NT	Pass**	Pass	???

♠ Q J 10 8 5 3   ♡ 9 5 3   ♢ 8 5 2   ♣ 7

Bid 2♠. The bridge logic for this bid is so clear that it shouldn't matter if partner took five minutes to pass! When East passed 1NT and you had only 3 HCP, North was marked with a good hand, regardless of whether or not he hesitated. **You did not benefit from his hesitation. That is the only issue.**

Passing with this hand is just as wrong as if your partner had opened 1NT. Bid with a clear conscience.

PRACTICE MAKES PERFECT

Bidding from hand records is a great way to fine-tune your partnership, and it's fun.

You don't even have to be in the same room. This works just as well over the phone or via e-mail. First, get two identical hand records from a bridge event in which you and your partner did not play. These can easily be found at tournaments and bridge clubs.

One player becomes "Northeast" and controls both the North and East cards. The other becomes "Southwest" and controls South and West. Each of you should cover up the two hands that belong to partner. Both players should record the auction using columns:

West   North   East   South

The dealer (designated on the hand record) begins the auction, just as if you were playing "real bridge." Observe the vulnerability (also designated). As the bidding progresses, focus on only one set of cards at a time. For example, when you are bidding North's cards, ignore East's cards. Continue the auction until there are three consecutive passes.

Once the auction is over, you can stop, see how you did, and discuss what happened. If you've ever wondered, "What would it have meant if I bid...," now's your chance to discuss it in detail.

At least one of you should also record any new agreements. For example, "Let's play --- as forcing," or "I'm surprised that you bid --- when vulnerable. Should I expect you to be very aggressive on these auctions?" Understanding your partner's style is even more important than knowing which conventions you have agreed to play. All partnership agreements should be recorded and saved on your computer or in some other manner.

Regardless of your level, it's a lot easier to play this game when you and partner are on the same page.

When partner's bid leads to a bad result, don't assume he made a mistake — it could just be the "luck of the cards."

You pick up ♠ K Q 4 3   ♡ 9   ◇ A K Q J 8   ♣ J 6 5

Your RHO opens 3♥, and you are pleased to double. Partner jumps to 4♠ — just what you were hoping for.

However, your joy is short-lived when the opponents:

Take the first three club tricks.	—	Bad news!
Fortunately, partner now claims.	—	Good news!
Down one, conceding the ♠A.	—	Terrible news!

How can this be? Not only did you have your double, but you would have been happy to double with less.

Would you now indicate your displeasure, and:

grab partner's cards to see what he had;	OR
ask partner why in the world he jumped;	OR
grab the traveler to see what others did;	OR
worst of all, do all of the above!!!	

I hope that you would do NONE OF THE ABOVE.
Instead, you should say, "Sorry my clubs weren't
better," or simply say nothing, pick up your next hand,
and move on. Here is the entire deal:

North

Contract: 4♠   ♠ K Q 4 3

Lead: ♣10   ♡ 9

                   ◇ A K Q J 8

                   ♣ J 6 5

West		*East*
♠ A 7		♠ 6
♡ Q J 10 8 7 4 2		♡ 5 3
◇ 7 4 3		◇ 10 9 6 5 2
♣ 10		♣ A K Q 8 3

South

           ♠ J 10 9 8 5 2

           ♡ A K 6

           ◇ —

           ♣ 9 7 4 2

West	*North*	*East*	*South*
3♡	Dbl	Pass	4♠
All Pass			

The right time to wheel out a convention is NOT in the middle of the auction.

One of the admirable traits of a winning player is that he avoids torturing partner. In a word, he's "practical." He never makes a bid that goes against his system or that he *hopes* partner will figure out — but might not.

West	North	East	South
Pass	1♣	Pass	1♠
Pass	1NT	Pass	???

♠ K Q 9 8 5   ♡ A 8 6   ♢ J 4   ♣ K J 2

If playing "New Minor Forcing," you would bid 2♢. This asks partner to show three-card support for your spades. You want to be in game, and if partner has three spades, you'd rather be in 4♠.

However, if you are not playing that convention with your present partner, or are unsure, or are afraid that partner might forget, don't risk 2♢. Simply raise to 3NT, and use the post-mortem to sort things out.

Chapter 2

Hand Evaluation

A Legend in His Own Mind

All of us could do a better job of evaluating their hands — even experts.

In the 2001 competition to determine the U.S. team in the world championships, an expert held:

♠ K 10 6   ♡ A 9 8   ◇ A 2   ♣ A K J 10 8

He opened 1♣, and after partner responded 1◇, he jumped to 2NT, showing 18-19 HCP and inviting game.

I was shocked!
Look at that great five-card suit.
Look at those lovely spot cards.
Look at all those prime cards (aces and kings).

How could he not upgrade his hand and open 2NT?
(At the other table, the player holding these cards appreciated this lovely hand, and did open 2NT.)

P.S. On the actual deal, nothing mattered. Partner had 8 HCP and raised to 3NT, which made easily.

P.P.S. Our "expert" lost the match.

THERE'S MORE TO LIFE THAN HCP

When raising partner's major, HCP are not the key — distribution points are.

Once you have a fit, short suits are just as valuable as high cards. Therefore, you should never think or say, "This raise promises --- HCP."

After partner opens 1♥ or 1♠

single raise   = 6 - 9 (or lousy 10) distribution points
limit raise   = 10 - 12   distribution points
forcing raise   = 13 +   distribution points
        distribution points = HCP + short-suit points

After partner opens 1♠

raise to 2♠ with these hands:

♠ 10 9 6   ♥ —   ◇ A 9 8 6 4   ♣ J 7 5 4 2
♠ 8 7 3   ♥ K J 7 3   ◇ J 6 3   ♣ K Q 6

make a limit raise with these hands:

♠ A 9 7 3   ♥ K 8 7 5   ◇ K 8   ♣ 6 4 2
♠ 10 8 7 6   ♥ K J 3   ◇ 3   ♣ A 9 8 6 3

make a forcing raise with these hands:

♠ Q J 9 4   ♥ A 9 6   ◇ A Q 8   ♣ 9 4 2
♠ 9 5 4 2   ♥ A 7   ◇ A K J 3   ♣ 9 7 6 2

Once partner raises your major suit, generously add points for trump length.

If your hand contains a singleton or void, add one point for a five-card trump suit.

Whether or not you have a short suit, add two additional points for each trump beyond five.
With: 6 trumps – add 2   7 trumps – add 4   (etc.)

Also, when your major is raised, add on for short suits:
        void – 3,   singleton – 2,   doubleton – 1

West	*North*	*East*	*South*
—	—	Pass	1♠
Pass	2♠	Pass	???

♠ K J 8 7 4 2   ♡ A 6   ◇ A Q 9 2   ♣ 8
Bid 4♠. 14 HCP + 3 (length) + 3 (shortness) = 20

♠ A 9 8 7 5 4 3   ♡ K J 3   ◇ 2   ♣ A 7
Bid 4♠. 12 HCP + 5 (length) + 3 (shortness) = 20

HONOR THY PARTNER

Honors in partner's long suit(s) are worth their weight in gold.

Once partner has shown a five-card suit, you should add a point for any honor (above the 10) in his suit. Don't add more than two points per hand.

Also worth knowing:

- No bonus for a singleton honor unless partner has shown at least a six-card suit.

- If partner has shown two long suits, you get bonus points for honors in each one.

- Opposite a six-card suit, the ace and king are invaluable. Take a second point for either one.

Partner opens 1♡. What is your hand worth now?

♠ 7 5   ♡ K 7 4   ◇ K Q 6 3   ♣ A 9 5 2
14 points. In addition to 12 HCP and a doubleton, you are entitled to add a point for the ♡K.

♠ K 7 4 2   ♡ J   ◇ A 7 5 4 3   ♣ 8 5 3
8 points. Don't add for the singleton ♡J unless partner rebids his suit.

North
♠ 5 4
♡ 7 2
◊ A Q 8 7 6 2
♣ A J 2

West
♠ Q J 10 7
♡ A Q 3
◊ J 3
♣ 9 8 5 3

East
♠ K 8 6
♡ K J 9 4
◊ 10 4
♣ Q 10 7 4

South
♠ A 9 3 2
♡ 10 8 6 5
◊ K 9 5
♣ K 6

West	*North*	*East*	*South*
—	1◊	Pass	1♡
Pass	2◊	Pass	???

With 10 HCP, most players would rebid 2NT or 3◊, but South realized that his ◊K was an absolute gem. He added two points for the high honor in North's six-card suit. Now that he had a "12" HCP hand opposite an opening bid, South lost no time bidding the laydown 3NT.

UP AND DOWN WE GO

Upgrade honor cards in RHO's suit.
Downgrade honor cards in LHO's suit.

Use the opponents' bidding to evaluate your hand.
You want your honors sitting "behind" their honors.

You are South, with this indifferent collection — 6 HCP
and flat as a pancake.

♠ K 8 2 ♡ K 6 4 ◇ 9 7 2 ♣ 8 6 5 3

West	North	East	South
1♣	1♠	2♡	???

Bid 2♠. Your ♡K is looking good "behind" the heart
bidder (East). With your two proven honors, you are
delighted to raise.

However, with the same hand after:

West	North	East	South
1♡	1♠	2♣	???

Pass. Now you're sitting "in front of" the heart bidder
(West), so the ♡K is not worth much.

Contract: 4♠
Lead: ♡7

North
♠ 9 8 5 4 3 2
♡ 5 3 2
♢ 7 6 3
♣ 6

West
♠ Q J
♡ 7
♢ K J 9 8 2
♣ J 9 8 4 2

East
♠ K
♡ K J 9 8 6 4
♢ A Q 10
♣ K 10 5

South
♠ A 10 7 6
♡ A Q 10
♢ 5 4
♣ A Q 7 3

West	North	East	South
—	—	—	1NT
Pass	2♡	Dbl	4♠!!!
All Pass			

Jumping to 4♠ after partner promised nothing "broke the rules." However, after East's lead-directing double, South loved his well-placed heart honors. Declarer won the heart lead and drew trumps. He later ruffed a club in dummy and finessed hearts. Making four.

Good hand evaluation can help any player make better slam decisions.

Contract: 6♠
Lead: ◇A

North
♠ A Q 9 7
♡ A 8 6 5 2
◇ K 5
♣ 6 3

West
♠ —
♡ Q 10 4 3
◇ A Q J 9 4 3
♣ K J 9

East
♠ J 10
♡ J 9
◇ 10 7 6 2
♣ Q 10 8 7 2

South
♠ K 8 6 5 4 3 2
♡ K 7
◇ 8
♣ A 5 4

West	*North*	*East*	*South*
—	1♡	Pass	1♠
2◇	3♠	Pass	4NT
Pass	5♡	Pass	6♠
All Pass			

North opened 1♡ with his 13 HCP. However, once
South responded 1♠ and West overcalled 2♢, North
took a second look at his hand. His ♢K now looked
awfully good, as did the honors in partner's spade suit.
With his four proven values, he upgraded his hand and
jumped to 3♠.

Once North showed support, South's spade suit looked
much better. He now re-evaluated his hand by adding:

> 5 length points for his seven-card suit;
>
> 1 point for the king in opener's suit;
>
> 3 points for a singleton and doubleton;

and when North showed two aces, South bid 6♠.

West led two rounds of diamonds, and South discarded
his ♣4 on dummy's ♢K. Declarer cashed two hearts
and led a third. East discarded a club and South ruffed
with the ♠2. South led a spade to dummy's queen, and
ruffed another heart, which pulled West's last heart.

It was now easy to lead a trump to dummy's ace, and
discard the ♣5 on North's last heart. Making six.

On a club lead, South would eventually discard his ♢8
on North's fifth heart, concede a club, and ruff a club.

With an independent major suit, don't even consider other contracts.

An independent suit is defined as a six-card (or longer) suit with at least four honors. With a normal trump split, you can draw trumps while losing at most one trump trick.

With the following hand, rebid 4♠ on each auction.

♠ A Q J 10 8 5   ♡ 2   ◇ 9 7 2   ♣ K Q 2

West	North	East	South
—	—	—	1♠
Pass	2◇	Pass	2♠
Pass	3NT	Pass	???

West	North	East	South
—	1♡	Pass	1♠
Pass	2◇	Pass	???

By the way: Occasionally, another contract might work out better. Nevertheless, insisting on your independent major suit will serve you very nicely.

With this great spade suit, South overruled his partner.

Contract: 4♠
Lead: ◇K

North
♠ 6
♡ A K 9 6 4 3
◇ 7 6 3
♣ A Q 4

West
♠ A 2
♡ 10 8
◇ K Q 10 9 5 2
♣ 8 6 2

East
♠ 9 8 5 3
♡ Q J 5 2
◇ J
♣ J 10 9 7

South
♠ K Q J 10 7 4
♡ 7
◇ A 8 4
♣ K 5 3

West	North	East	South
—	—	—	1♠
3◇	3♡	Pass	3♠
Pass	4♡	Pass	4♠
All Pass			

4♠ made five. South discarded a diamond on the ♡K, and lost one diamond and one spade. In 4♡, North would lose two hearts, two diamonds, and one spade.

Overrated Jacks

Jacks are the most overrated of honors. "Jackless" hands should be upgraded.

No one is saying that jacks are worthless. However, you'll definitely take more tricks with hands that don't contain "too many" jacks.

West	North	East	South
—	—	Pass	1NT
Pass	2♣	Pass	2♠
Pass	3♠	Pass	???

♠ K Q J 3 ♡ K J 8 ◇ Q J 7 4 ♣ K J
Pass. 17 HCP and a doubleton. However, look at all those jacks. Yuck.

♠ K Q 9 3 ♡ A Q 8 ◇ K Q 7 4 ♣ 7 5
Bid 4♠. Not a jack in sight.

♠ A 10 9 3 ♡ A 10 8 ◇ A K 9 4 ♣ 7 5
Bid 4♠. Some would call this a 15 HCP minimum. However, where I come from, no jacks, two tens and four quick tricks make this a 15 HCP maximum!

With "only" 16 HCP, most North players would invite slam by responding 4NT. However, our hero upgraded his jackless hand and jumped to 6NT.

North

Contract: 6NT
Lead: ♠J

♠ 8 2
♡ A 7 4
♢ A Q 10 2
♣ A Q 6 3

West
♠ J 10 9 7
♡ J 2
♢ 9 6 5
♣ J 9 8 5

East
♠ K Q 5 4 3
♡ 9 8 6 5
♢ J 7 3
♣ 10

South
♠ A 6
♡ K Q 10 3
♢ K 8 4
♣ K 7 4 2

West	North	East	South
—	—	Pass	1NT
Pass	6NT	All Pass	

Despite the bad club split, everyone took 12 tricks. But with only 31 HCP, very few pairs got to slam.

NOT ALL 15'S ARE CREATED EQUAL

Don't open 1NT with 15 **ugly** HCP.

Take a look at the following:

♠ Q 7　♡ K J 6 4　◇ K J 6　♣ K Q 5 3

♠ K Q 5　♡ K J　◇ Q 7 5 3　♣ K J 6 2

♠ K Q J　♡ K 6 5 4　◇ Q J　♣ Q J 7 4

These are balanced hands with 15 HCP, but I would downgrade all of them, and open 1♣. Why?

- no aces
- too many jacks
- no useful nines and tens
- too many honors in short suits
- no five-card suit

Whether you're an optimist or a pessimist,
**always upgrade hands with "good" honor cards,
but downgrade hands with "bad" honor cards.**

Chapter 3

Opener's Decisions

6-5, COME ALIVE

With 6-5 distribution and a minimum opening bid, open your five-card suit when it is higher-ranking.

West	North	East	South
—	—	Pass	???

♠ 7   ♡ A K 9 6 4   ◇ 2   ♣ K 10 8 7 6 3

Open 1♡. If partner responds 1♠, you have an easy 2♣ rebid. A 1♣ opening bid would not leave you well-placed, because you can hardly reverse with only 10 HCP.

♠ 7   ♡ A K 9 6 4   ◇ 2   ♣ A K 10 8 7 6

Open 1♣. You plan to reverse into hearts and then rebid that suit. That will tell partner that you have a big hand with five hearts and therefore six clubs (you would obviously open 1♡ with 5-5).

♠ K Q 9 7 2   ♡ A J 7 5 4 2   ◇ 6   ♣ 3

Open 1♠ with this minimum opening bid.

♠ A K Q 9 7   ♡ A Q 9 5 4 2   ◇ 6   ♣ 3

Open 1♡ with this terrific opening bid.

To Rebid or Not to Rebid?

In general, opener should not rebid a five-card suit. However, there are five logical exceptions.

1. Partner supports your suit.
2. Partner guarantees at least a doubleton in your suit.
3. Partner promises another bid.
4. A competitive auction leaves you no alternative.
5. Your suit contains four honors.

West	North	East	South
—	—	—	1♠
Pass	2♠	Pass	???

♠ A Q J 8 2 ♡ 9 ◇ K Q 9 7 ♣ K Q J
Rebid 4♠, obviously. (exception #1)

West	North	East	South
—	—	—	1♣
Pass	1NT	Pass	???

♠ K Q 9 6 ♡ 7 ◇ Q 6 4 ♣ K Q 10 8 6
Rebid 2♣, obviously. (exception #2)

West	North	East	South
—	—	—	1♢
Pass	1♡	Pass	1♠
Pass	2♣	Pass	???

♠ A J 5 2   ♡ 5 3   ♢ A K 9 7 4   ♣ 4 2

Rebid 2♢. Some pairs treat North's bid of the fourth suit as game-forcing; others can stop below game. In either case, partner can't pass 2♢. (exception #3)

West	North	East	South
—	—	Pass	1♣
1♠	2♡	Pass	???

♠ 8 7 4 2   ♡ A   ♢ A Q 5   ♣ Q J 10 9 2

Rebid 3♣, grateful that your suit is as good as it is. (exception #4)

West	North	East	South
—	—	Pass	1♡
Pass	1NT	Pass	???

♠ A K J 9   ♡ K Q J 10 8   ♢ 6 5 2   ♣ 4

Rebid 2♡. Whether or not you play "1NT Forcing," this is the logical bid. (exception # 5)

**If the thought of being passed out in
1♡ or 1♠ would make you ill, open 2♣.**

All you need is the potential to win nine tricks with
your long suit as trumps, including at least four
quick tricks. HCP are not the key.

This hand clearly qualifies:

♠ 9 5   ♡ A K Q J 8 7   ◇ A K J 10   ♣ 5

With hearts as trumps, you will win six heart tricks,
and at least three diamonds. Your ♡A K and ◇A K
satisfy the four quick-trick requirement. Any outraged
reader who complains, "You can't open 2♣ with only
18 HCP," deserves to be passed out in 1♡ when all
partner has is the ◇Q.

Here are two hands from recent high-level competition
which demonstrate that even experts don't open 2♣ as
often as they should.

On the first hand, both pairs missed a laydown slam.

West	West	East	East
♠ K Q 10 8 6 4 2	1♠	1NT	♠ A 9
♡ A 2	3♣	3♢	♡ J 7 4
♢ A	3♠	4♠	♢ K 8 7 3 2
♣ K Q 3	Pass		♣ J 10 2

Why didn't West open 2♣? What was he waiting for? All he needed to make 4♠ was a pair of black jacks.

3♣, what a "lovely" bid! Both West players chose this bid because they thought they were too strong to jump to 4♠. This sounds like they were confessing, "I should have opened 2♣."

On the next hand, E-W missed a laydown game.

West	West	East	East
♠ A K	1♡	Pass	♠ Q J 10 9 2
♡ A 9 6 4 3 2			♡ 8 7 5
♢ J			♢ 8 4
♣ A K Q 6			♣ J 7 4

When will they ever learn?

A 2♣ opening bid is not forcing to game.
You can stop in 2NT, 3 of a major,
4 of a minor, or double the opponents.

In these four examples, 2♦ is a waiting bid.

West	West	East	East
♠ K Q 10 7	2♣	2♦	♠ 6 3
♡ K J	2NT	Pass	♡ 9 7 5 3
♢ A Q J			♢ 9 8 4 2
♣ A K 7 4			♣ 8 5 2

With East's yarborough, a 2NT contract is high enough.

West	West	East	East
♠ J 4 3	2♣	2♦	♠ 8 6 5 2
♡ A K Q J 9 7 4	2♡	3♣*	♡ 5
♢ 9	3♡	Pass	♢ J 5 3 2
♣ A K			♣ 9 8 7 5

*3♣ = second negative (0-3 HCP).

West's bidding shows a nine-trick hand, and invites
East to raise if he has a trick. With a hand that's better
for poker (four of a kind), East declines.

West	West	East	East
♠ 9	2♣	2♦	♠ J 8 5 4 2
♡ 8 2	3♣	3♦*	♡ J 7 4 3
◇ A K Q	4♣	Pass	◇ 9 3
♣ A K Q J 8 6 5			♣ 7 4

*3◇ = second negative (0-3 HCP).

West says he needs some help to make 5♣.
By now, East is sorry he got out of bed.

West	W	N	E	S	East
♠ A Q 3	2♣	Pass	2◇	3♣	♠ 9 7 5 4
♡ A 6	Dbl	All Pass			♡ Q 9 7 4
◇ A K 8 5					◇ 6 4 2
♣ A J 9 7					♣ 5 3

West is delighted to double 3♣. East is happy to pass opener's penalty double. South won't enjoy playing 3♣ doubled.

By the way: If responder bids anything other than a "second negative," the auction becomes game-forcing.

A MAJESTIC DOUBLE JUMP

After you open and partner bids a suit at the one level, your double jump to 3NT guarantees at least a six-card suit.

Obviously, this bid also promises a very strong hand with stoppers in the unbid suits. If partner has a suitable hand, he is welcome to bid on.

Why can't you have a balanced hand for your 3NT bid? With a balanced hand and 18-19 HCP, you'd jump to 2NT. With 20 balanced HCP, you would open 2NT.

Why can't opener have only a five-card suit? Every unbalanced hand with a five-card suit must include a second suit — and you would have bid it.

West	North	East	South
—	—	—	1♦
Pass	1♡	Pass	???

Rebid 3NT with each of these hands.

♠ K 10 ♡ 9 ◇ A K Q 10 8 6 3 ♣ A 7 3

♠ A J 9 ♡ Q 9 ◇ A Q J 7 6 2 ♣ K Q

DOUBLE JUMP...CONTINUED

Contract: 6♣
Lead: ♣10

North
♠ A
♡ 8 4 3
◇ K 9 7 5 4 2
♣ Q 8 2

West
♠ K J 9 2
♡ J 7 6
◇ A 10 8 6
♣ 10 9

East
♠ 8 7 5 4 3
♡ Q 10 5 2
◇ Q J 3
♣ 7

South
♠ Q 10 6
♡ A K 9
◇ —
♣ A K J 6 5 4 3

West	North	East	South
—	—	Pass	1♣
Pass	1◇	Pass	3NT
Pass	4♠	Pass	6♣
All Pass			

South showed great clubs and a great hand with 3NT. North loved his singleton spade and club support, and cue-bid 4♠. 6♣ was easy — South ruffed two spades.

Which minor should you open with 4-4 and a balanced hand? Who cares?

This is true whether you have 12-14 HCP or 18-19 HCP (too strong to open 1NT).

Too many players believe that it's important to open 1 ♢ so that they can rebid 2 ♣ without reversing. However, that's silly. When you open 1 ♣ or 1 ♢ with 4-4 in the minors and a balanced hand, you won't have any rebid problems — you'll just bid notrump.

I suggest opening the stronger suit. But opening 1 ♢ Mondays, Wednesdays, and Fridays, and 1 ♣ on any other day, is almost as good. Whatever!

By the way: When opener has 4-4 in the minors and an *unbalanced* hand, it is usually sensible to open 1 ♢. However, I refuse to open 1 ♢ and rebid 2 ♣ with a terrible 4-card diamond suit. With a hand such as:

♠ J ♡ A J 9 7 ♢ J 6 4 2 ♣ A Q 9 2

I open 1 ♣ and rebid 1NT after 1 ♠.

Chapter 4

Responder's
Decisions

The Unbalanced Notrump

A 1NT response can be made on a very unbalanced hand.

A response at the two level in a new suit shows at least 10 HCP. Therefore, after an opening bid of 1$\diamond$, 1$\heartsuit$, or 1$\spadesuit$, many weak hands must respond 1NT, even with very unbalanced distribution.

♠ Q 7 ♡ K ◇ J 7 3 ♣ Q 9 7 6 5 4 2
Respond 1NT to an opening bid of 1◇, 1♡ or 1♠.

♠ Q J 6 ♡ — ◇ A Q 8 6 4 ♣ 8 7 5 4 2
Respond 1NT to an opening bid of 1♡.

♠ 8 ♡ 9 3 ◇ K 9 7 6 5 4 ♣ K 9 8 7
Respond 1NT to an opening bid of 1♡ or 1♠.

♠ 3 ♡ K 8 7 5 3 2 ◇ Q 8 5 2 ♣ Q 6
Respond 1NT to an opening bid of 1♠.

On the other hand: If partner opens 1♣, responder can easily show any new suit at the one level, so a 1NT response guarantees a balanced hand.

One of the best (and easiest) of the competitive conventions is responder's Weak Jump Raise (WJR).

Responder promises a fit for partner's suit and a weak hand. This preemptive bid is based on The LAW of Total Tricks: **you are *always* safe in bidding to the level of your side's number of trumps.**

Once you know that you have a nine-card fit, don't be afraid to compete to the three level, even with very weak hands. With ten trumps, it's usually correct to make a WJR to the four level.

Here are three of the most common auctions where the WJR can be used.

1. Partner opens one (of any suit) and RHO doubles;

2. Partner opens one (of any suit) and RHO overcalls;

3. Partner overcalls, no matter what RHO does next.

By the way: With good support and 10+ distribution points, responder should cue-bid the opponent's suit.

♠ 9 6 5 3   ♡ 8 6   ◇ K 9 7 5 4   ♣ 6 3

With a hand like this, South should WJR partner's suit
to the three level on each of these eight auctions,
regardless of vulnerability:

West	North	East	South
Pass	1♠	Dbl	???
—	1◇	Dbl	???
—	1♠	2♣	???
Pass	1◇	1♡	???
—	1◇	1NT	???
1◇	1♠	Dbl	???
1♡	1♠	2♡	???
1♣	1♠	Pass	???

On the following, once North overcalls in diamonds,
you know your side has a 10-card fit, so jump to 4◇:

West	North	East	South
1♣	1◇	2NT	???
1♡	2◇	2♠	???

BID MORE WITH LESS

When partner opens and your RHO doubles or overcalls, responder's jump-shift should be preemptive.

The Weak Jump-Shift (WJS) in competition shows a long suit and a weak hand. How weak? Suit quality, level, and vulnerability are all relevant.

Responder typically holds:
at the two level: a six-card suit with 3-6 HCP
at the three level: six or seven cards with 3-7 HCP.

West	North	East	South
—	1♣	Dbl	???

♠ 6 5 3   ♡ K J 10 9 6 3   ◇ 7   ♣ 8 4 2
Bid 2♡ at any vulnerability with this textbook hand.

♠ 9 5 2   ♡ 7 2   ◇ A 9 8 7 5 3   ♣ 7 4
With this indifferent suit, jump to 2◇ only when you're not vulnerable.

♠ 6 2   ♡ A K 10 7 6 5   ◇ 8 7 3   ♣ 6 4
Bid 1♡. Too strong for a WJS.

West	North	East	South
Pass	1♢	1♡	???

♠ Q J 10 9 8 4   ♡ 6 4   ♢ 7 5   ♣ 8 4 2
Jump to 2♠ at any vulnerability. Topless long suits with nice "fillers" make perfect preempts.

♠ 9 2   ♡ 7 2   ♢ 8 6 4   ♣ K J 10 8 6 3
Jump to 3♣ only if nonvulnerable. Avoid vulnerable preempts at the three level unless you have a great suit.

♠ 9 2   ♡ 7 2   ♢ 8 6 4   ♣ K Q J 10 9 6
Bid 3♣ at any vulnerability. This is a GREAT suit.

♠ Q 10 8 7 5 4 2   ♡ 6 2   ♢ 5 3   ♣ Q 4
Jump to 2♠. Treating a weak seven-card suit as a six-bagger is very sensible.

♠ A J 10 9 6 5   ♡ 6   ♢ 10 9 4 3   ♣ 9 7
Bid 1♠. This hand is definitely too strong for a WJS. 6-4 hands tend to take a lot of tricks, especially when partner has bid your four-card suit.

STAND TALL AFTER A 1NT OVERCALL

If partner opens and RHO overcalls 1NT, your only strong action is a penalty double.

After partner opens, you can double a 1NT overcall with as few as 9 HCP, because you know your side has the "balance of power." Therefore, you're happy to bid (or even jump) with weak distributional hands. If you don't double, opener will know that you have less than 9 HCP. With a shapely hand, you should try to bid. Defending 1NT is never any fun.

West	North	East	South
—	1♢	1NT	???

♠ J 10 9 6   ♡ Q 6 4   ♢ K 4   ♣ A 7 5 2
Double. You don't have to worry about where your tricks are coming from. The key is that E-W will have no chance to make seven tricks based on your 10 HCP and partner's opening bid.

♠ 5   ♡ 7 6   ♢ 7 4 2   ♣ Q J 10 9 6 5 4
Preempt 3♣. Force them to search for their major-suit fit(s) at the three level.

♠ Q 7 4 3   ♡ K 7 4 2   ◇ 4   ♣ K 7 5 2

Pass. Your side may very well have a fit, but there is no way to find it. No one ever said that you are obligated to respond with 8 HCP *after an overcall.*

♠ Q 8 6 5 2   ♡ 4 3   ◇ J 10 3 2   ♣ A 7

Bid 2◇. Your spades are too weak to bid. If North has a singleton spade, you could be in big trouble. Partner almost certainly has at least four diamonds, so "support with support."

♠ K J 10 9 7 6   ♡ 7 4 3   ◇ 8 6   ♣ 5 3

Bid 2♠. You would be delighted to play in 2♠, or push the opponents to the three level. You won't be thrilled if partner tables a singleton spade, but your suit is strong enough to survive.

By the way: We've all encountered players who believe that responder's double of a 1NT overcall is negative. This is neither logical nor standard. **Negative doubles are only used after a natural overcall in a suit.**

In general, responder should not rebid a five-card suit. However, there are four logical exceptions.

1. Opener supports your suit.
2. Opener guarantees at least a doubleton in your suit.
3. Opener reverses.
4. Your suit contains four honors.

West	North	East	South
Pass	1♦	Pass	1♥
Pass	2♥	Pass	???

♠ A Q 4   ♥ K 10 8 7 4   ♦ Q 9 7 3   ♣ 8
Rebid 4♥, obviously. (exception #1)

West	North	East	South
—	1♣	Pass	1♥
Pass	1NT	Pass	???

♠ K 6 4 3   ♥ Q J 9 8 5   ♦ 7   ♣ 6 5 3
Rebid 2♥. (exception #2)

West	North	East	South
Pass	1♣	Pass	1♠
Pass	2♡	Pass	???

♠ A Q 10 8 6 ♡ A 4 2 ◇ 5 4 3 ♣ K 4

Rebid 2♠. Slam is a distinct possibility, and you want to explore by making an economical bid. After his reverse, opener owes you another bid. (exception #3)

West	North	East	South
—	1◇	Pass	1♡
Pass	2♣	Pass	???

♠ 6 5 3 2 ♡ A K J 10 9 ◇ J ♣ 8 3 2

Rebid 2♡. Game is still possible, so you shouldn't pass. If partner has to pass 2♡ with a singleton, your guaranteed four trump winners will see you through the 5-1 "fit." (exception #4)

UP THE LINE — NO THANKS

If partner opens 1♣, and you have diamonds and a major, respond in the major.

No matter how fond you are of diamonds in real life, in bridge they are not an important suit. Informing opener that you have diamonds will not help him.

West	North	East	South
—	1♣	Pass	???

♠ 7 ♡ K 9 6 4 ◇ K 9 6 4 ♣ 8 7 4 2

Respond 1♡. Tell partner about your major while it's easy to do so. If you respond 1◇, you could easily lose a heart fit if West bids spades.

♠ A 10 8 4 ♡ Q 7 ◇ A 7 6 5 3 ♣ 9 6

Respond 1♠. Yes, you have more diamonds than spades. So what! You're not interested in a 5◇ contract. The fact that you have 10 HCP rather than 6 HCP changes nothing.

Important exception: If your diamonds are longer than your major *and* you have an opening bid or better, respond 1◇.

BID MORE WITH MORE

With a good hand, respond naturally — longest suit first. When your hand is weak or mediocre, you don't have that luxury.

West	North	East	South
Pass	1♦	Pass	???

♠ A K 7 2 ♡ 6 4 ◇ 7 6 ♣ A K 9 6 3

Respond 2♣. Although you are more interested in your major, you should wait until your next turn to show it. You want partner to know that you have exactly four spades. If you respond 1♠ and later bid clubs, partner will have every right to place you with five spades, and will support you with three.

♠ 9 7 4 3 ♡ 6 4 ◇ 7 6 ♣ A Q J 10 9

Respond 1♠. Your clubs are lovely, but with only 7 HCP, a 2♣ response is out of the question.

♠ Q 7 4 3 ♡ Q 6 ◇ J 3 ♣ A Q 6 4 2

Respond 1♠. Your 11 HCP allow you to respond at the two level. However, with this mediocre hand, you've got to be practical — so show your most important suit now.

If partner opens a minor and you have: good support, VOB or better, but no good bid – temporize by bidding the other minor.

Advocates of Inverted Minors have no problem here. They treat a raise to two of opener's minor as forcing, showing at least 10 HCP. However, for everyone else, these hands can be a real problem.

The lesser-of-evils answer is to respond in the unbid minor. Partner is very unlikely to get carried away supporting *that* suit. This might not be true if you lied by bidding a major.

Should you show support for opener's minor suit later on? That will depend on how the auction develops.

With both of these hands, respond 1♦ to 1♣:
♠ A 5 3 ♡ 7 6 4 ♦ 9 5 4 ♣ A K Q 5
♠ A 7 ♡ 8 4 ♦ A 4 2 ♣ K J 9 6 5 3

With both of these hands, respond 2♣ to 1♦:
♠ J 6 4 ♡ 10 9 5 ♦ A K J 2 ♣ A 9 7
♠ A 8 2 ♡ K 2 ♦ A K Q 10 8 ♣ J 6 3

Chapter 5

Notrump Bidding

STAYMAN YES, JACOBY NO

If partner opens 1NT, and you have 5-4 in the majors and a game-going hand (9+ HCP), do not transfer. Instead, respond 2♣.

This is true for hands with four spades and five hearts, or five spades and four hearts.

What should responder do next?

If opener bids a major, raise him to game.

If opener bids 2♢, force to game by jumping in your five-card major. With a doubleton in your five-bagger, opener will bid 3NT. If he has three-card support, he will usually raise, but if he has terrific minors, he may elect to bid 3NT.

By the way: After responding 2♣, "Smolen" players jump in their four-card suit (alertable), which guarantees that opener will become declarer.

By the way #2: Because all game-forcing hands with 5-4 in the majors respond with 2♣, the following useful inference is available. If responder transfers to spades and then bids 3♡, he must have **five** hearts.

Only Slightly Unbalanced

Opening 1NT with two doubletons is neither illegal nor unwise.

Because it's so descriptive, I like to open 1NT as often as possible. This also avoids nasty rebid problems that may be unavoidable if you opened in a suit.

Yes, you could certaily describe opening 1NT with two doubletons as "unorthodox." No, I would not teach this technique to beginners. But for everyone else, I heartily recommend it.

When considering opening 1NT with 5-4-2-2:

Having strength in your short suits is helpful, but not mandatory. Don't let a worthless doubleton stop you.

With 5-4-2-2 and a five-card major, open in the major.

I add one point for a five-card suit in notrump, so I will open 1NT with 5-4-2-2 and an attractive 14 HCP. I describe this by writing and announcing: "14+ to 17" for a 1NT opening bid.

West	North	East	South
—	—	Pass	???

♠ K J ♡ A J 6 4 ◇ A 10 8 6 2 ♣ K 3

Open 1NT. If you open 1◇, you'll be stuck after a 1♠ response — you're not strong enough to jump to 2NT, or make a 2♡ reverse, and a 1NT rebid shows 12-14 HCP. If you open 1NT, your next bid will be easy.

♠ J 4 ♡ A K 10 2 ◇ J 6 ♣ A Q 10 7 3

Open 1NT. Although your short suits are stopperless, before you open the "obvious" 1♣, ask yourself, "What will I rebid after the likely 1♠ response?" 1NT is a big underbid, so avoid the problem and open 1NT.

♠ K 10 6 ♡ K 7 ◇ K J ♣ A J 7 6 5 3

Open 1NT — okay when you have a six-card minor. **You never want to open 1NT with a six-card major.** All of your honors in the other suits are crying out: "Our hand must become declarer to protect against the opening lead coming through us."

A Minor Inconvenience

After opening 1NT, every pair needs a way for responder to sign off in 3♣ or 3♦.

Although everyone knows how responder can escape from 1NT into a major, sometimes he needs to escape into a minor suit.

Obviously, when playing Stayman and Jacoby, you can't show your minor suit at the two level. Therefore, you must have a way to bail out in 3 of a minor with hands such as:

♠ 8 7   ♡ 7   ◇ 10 7 5 4   ♣ Q 9 8 7 4 2

♠ 7   ♡ 8 5 4   ◇ Q J 10 8 6 3   ♣ 8 4 3

Notice that both examples contain six-card suits. Opener may have a doubleton, so you do not want to risk playing at the three level with seven trumps. With a hand like:

♠ 8 6 3   ♡ 9   ◇ K 8 5 4 2   ♣ 7 5 4 2
Pass 1NT and wish partner luck.

Here are three ways for responder to sign off in 3♣
or 3♢. Select one only. Don't lose sleep about
which method is "best," or who will become declarer.
All that matters is that you and your partner have an
agreement that both players can easily remember.

Direct jump to 3♣ or 3♢. Opener will alert as a
"signoff," and pass without looking at his hand.

"Faking Stayman." Some pairs have agreed that
responder can bid Stayman without a four-card major,
as long as he follows up with a 3♣ or 3♢ signoff.
At this point, opener must alert by saying (if asked),
"Responder is signing off, and may not have a major."

"Four-Suit Transfers" are becoming more popular.
There are a few variations. I prefer to play that 2♠
promises clubs, and 2NT promises a diamond suit.
All transfers must be announced. The 2♠ and 2NT
responses can also be made with strong hands.

By the way: When playing Four-Suit Transfers, and
2NT would promise diamonds, you can't make an
immediate, natural raise to 2NT. The solution is to
respond 2♣, and then rebid 2NT (alertable).

To Bid or Not to Bid

If RHO bids or doubles after partner's Jacoby Transfer, you don't have to bid.

Of course, the 1NT opener may choose to bid with a fit and a suitable hand. However, you must be discreet; after all, responder did not promise any strength.

West	North	East	South
—	—	—	1NT
Pass	2♡*	3♣	???

*transfer to spades

♠ A 8 5　♡ A Q 2　◇ K J 7 2　♣ Q 7 3
Pass. Yes, you have a spade fit, but this is only a so-so hand in support of spades.

♠ Q 8 3 2　♡ A K Q 6　◇ A 10 7　♣ 5 3
Bid 3♠. This is a terrific hand for spades.

♠ A 5　♡ 8 6 4 2　◇ A K 7　♣ A Q 8 7
Double. Even if partner has nothing, you expect to defeat 3♣.

West	North	East	South
—	—	—	1NT
Pass	2♡*	Dbl	???

♠ Q 9 7   ♡ K 8 2   ◇ Q J 3   ♣ A K 9 7

Bid 2♠. This promises spade support. With only two spades, you would pass East's lead-directing double.

♠ K Q 7 5   ♡ A 2   ◇ A 9 2   ♣ K 10 8 3

Jump to 3♠, just as you would if East had passed.

♠ K 2   ♡ K 9 6   ◇ K Q 8 7   ♣ A J 7 4

Pass, the normal action here with a doubleton in your partner's suit. Telling partner that you don't like his suit may not be good news, but it is very relevant information. If partner has a weak hand, he can bid 2♠ himself or force you to bid 2♠ by redoubling.

♠ K 2   ♡ A J 10 8   ◇ A 10 9 3   ♣ A 10 7

Redouble, showing heart length and strength. Partner is welcome to pass with some hearts and some points.

Warning: Not everyone defines "redouble" on these auctions as I have described above. Instead of assuming that you know what partner thinks, ask him.

DECISIONS, DECISIONS

You open 1NT, and partner transfers and invites game by bidding 2NT. You now have four options.

Responder has a five-card major and 8-9 HCP. He usually has a balanced hand.

West	North	East	South
—	—	—	1NT
Pass	2♡*	Pass	2♠
Pass	2NT	Pass	???

*Jacoby Transfer

♠ 7 5　♡ A K J 4　♢ Q J 5　♣ A 7 4 3
Pass — minimum hand with only two spades.

♠ A 6 3　♡ 6 4 2　♢ A K 5　♣ K J 4 2
Sign off in 3♠ — minimum hand with spade support.

♠ K 6　♡ K Q 5　♢ A Q J 3　♣ Q 9 6 2
Raise to 3NT — maximum hand with only two spades.

♠ A Q 9　♡ A J 10 4　♢ 8 3　♣ K Q 7 2
Jump to 4♠ — maximum hand with spade support.

Chapter 6

Better
Slam Decisions

SLIM AND NONE

After a limit raise, opener should not consider slam without a singleton or void.

Responder's limit raise shows 11-ish points. Even after re-evaluating, opener needs 22 points to total 33. He won't have that many HCP after opening a one-bid. A very strong hand is not enough; opener also needs great shape.

West	North	East	South
—	—	—	1♡
Pass	3♡	Pass	???

♠ J 8 ♡ A K Q J 7 ◇ A Q 5 ♣ K J 2
Bid 4♡. 21 HCP, but you have too many holes to fill.

♠ A Q ♡ K Q J 9 8 6 ◇ K J ♣ Q 6 3
Bid 4♡. Slam chances are too slim to worry about; partner would need "the perfect hand." Forget about it.

♠ A K 10 4 ♡ A Q 9 8 5 3 ◇ A 5 ♣ 4
Cue-bid 3♠ with this lovely 6-4 hand that includes three first-round controls.

When responder wants to make a forcing raise in opener's major, Jacoby 2NT is an excellent convention to explore for slam.

The 2NT bid (alertable) promises four trumps and 13+ points including distribution, with no upper limit. Responder's hand is usually balanced. However, both players must know what happens next.

Opener rebids after a Jacoby 2NT response:
(all bids are alertable)

With a singleton or void, opener bids his short suit at the three level. His bid says nothing about the strength of his hand. If he has a strong five-card side suit and a minimum opening bid, he can convey that information by jumping in his second suit.

With no singleton or void, opener will define his strength with an artificial bid. Each of these reflect points after re-evaluating (assume 1♡ was opened).

3♡ = 18+   3NT = 15-17   4♡ = 12-14
Notice that the cheaper the bid, the better the hand.

West	West	East	East
♠ A Q 7 6 4	1♠	2NT*	♠ K J 9 5
♡ K 8 5	4♠*	Pass	♡ A Q 7 2
◇ Q J 3			◇ 7 4 2
♣ J 9	*alertable bid		♣ A K

East had visions of sugarplums after West opened 1♠. However, when West showed a minimum, balanced hand with his 4♠ rebid, East wisely called it a day.

West	West	East	East
♠ A J 10 4 3	1♠	2NT*	♠ K 9 8 5 2
♡ 7	3♡*	4♣	♡ 9 8 4
◇ A J 9 2	4◇	4NT	◇ K 8
♣ Q 8 7	5♡	6♠	♣ A K J
	Pass		

*alertable bid

West's 3♡ bid showed a singleton or void. This was music to East's ears — he couldn't lose more than one heart trick. East cue-bid 4♣ to show his club control. West didn't have a great opening bid, but it was easy to cue-bid 4◇. That was all East needed to hear. When West showed two aces, East bid the laydown slam.

Patience is a Virtue

If partner opens 2♣, respond 2♦ unless you have a suit that is *both* long and strong.

When partner shows a great hand, you are delighted to have "points." After all, everyone loves a slam. However, there's no hurry to tell partner the good news. Opener usually has his own suit, so let him go first. For now, just make a waiting bid of 2♦.

If you have a suit worth talking about, that's different. You need 8+ HCP, and at least a five-card suit with two of the top three honors, or three of the top five.

Nevertheless, your priorities should vary depending on which suit you have. In response to 2♣:

3♣: A delayed 3♣ bid is artificial. With clubs, it's now or never.   Highest priority

2♡: The cheapest positive response.   High priority

2♠: Awkward if opener has hearts.   Lower priority

3♦: The least economical positive.   Lowest priority

West	North	East	South
Pass	2♣	Pass	???

♠ 9 5 2   ♡ 8 7 3   ◇ A K J   ♣ Q 9 6 4

Bid 2◇. Some players add up their 10 HCP, and act like they have "ants in their pants" by responding 2NT. This impatient bid prevents opener from bidding a major at the two level, and insures that the strong hand will become the dummy in a notrump contract.

♠ Q 9 5 4   ♡ A 4   ◇ A Q 7 5 2   ♣ 10 8

Bid 2◇. A lot of points, an adequate suit, but jumping to 3◇ would crowd the auction. You're on your way to slam — now let's explore for the best trump suit.

♠ 8 5   ♡ A Q J 10 8 5   ◇ 8 4   ♣ 6 5 3

Bid 2♡. Only 7 HCP, but who cares? You're dying to talk about this suit, so bid it.

♠ A J 7 5 4   ♡ K 7   ◇ Q 9 5 3   ♣ J 4

Bid 2◇. Another nice hand with scattered values and a suit that can wait.

♠ K 8 5 4   ♡ 7 5   ◇ 5 3   ♣ K Q J 9 8

Bid 3♣. Show your excellent suit while you can.

When partner invites a notrump slam with a jump to 4NT, you are welcome to bid a suit.

After a quantitative 4NT, most players believe that your only options are pass and 6NT. That's too inflexible. 12 tricks are always easier with a trump suit. Why not look for a fit? If partner doesn't like your suit, he can bid his own suit or return to notrump.

West	West	East	East
♠ 7 4	1NT	4NT	♠ A K 9
♡ K 8 3	5♣	5♢	♡ A Q J
♢ K Q J 4	6♢	Pass	♢ 10 9 8 5 2
♣ A K 5 2			♣ J 6

After 1NT, East correctly evaluated his 15 HCP and five-card suit as being worthy of a slam invitation. West's spades suggested a suit contract, so he decided to look for a minor-suit slam. By bidding his cheaper minor, he expected to find a fit — once East did not bid Stayman, he had to have a minor.

East didn't like clubs, but was happy to mention his diamonds. 6♢ was ice-cold, while 6NT had no chance.

West	West	East	East
♠ K 8	1NT	2♡*	♠ Q 6 5 4 2
♡ K 8 3	2♠	4NT	♡ A Q 9
◇ J 4 2	6♣	Pass	◇ A K
♣ A K Q 10 7			♣ J 9 2

*Jacoby Transfer

After transferring, East's 4NT bid was quantitative, inviting slam in spades or notrump. It would not have been crazy for West to bid 6NT, but there was no hurry. His club suit was certainly worth mentioning.

West jumped to 6♣ to emphasize his great suit. If partner hated clubs, he was welcome to bid 6NT.

Clubs were okay with East. If West had two spades, East's weak spade suit rated to be useless in notrump.

6♣ presented no problems. West won the diamond lead and unblocked East's other honor. Declarer returned to his hand and ruffed his last diamond with the 9♣. He drew trumps and conceded a spade trick.

Every other pair in the room played 6NT, down one.

YOU DON'T NEED TO BE FIRST

A "slam try" cue-bid promises first OR second-round control in that suit.

Many players think that first-round control is a must. Not so. Second-round control (king or singleton) is perfectly adequate. After all, you still have room to sort things out with Blackwood.

West	North	East	South
—	1♢	1♠	2♡
3♣	3♡	Pass	???

♠ K 8 ♡ A K Q 10 4 ♢ A Q 4 ♣ 7 6 2

Cue-bid 3♠. You are dying to learn if partner has a control in clubs. After your economical 3♠ cue-bid, it will be easy for partner to show a club control (bid 4♣), or deny one (bid 4♢ or 4♡).

♠ 8 7 ♡ A Q J 9 8 6 4 ♢ A Q 6 ♣ 7

Cue-bid 4♣. This will tell partner the following: you're interested in slam, clubs are not a problem, but spades are (no 3♠ cue-bid). Who can ask for more?

Chapter 7

Preempts
for
Fun & Profit

ENJOYING GOING TOPLESS

The most attractive suit for an opening three-bid is topless, but nicely filled out.

Q J 10 9 8 7 6 is an excellent trump suit. It provides five guaranteed winners even if partner is void. The opponents' only potential winners are the two top honors. If any other suit becomes trump, your suit is useless. Therefore, if you're lucky enough to hold a suit like this one, you should bend over backwards to make it the trump suit.

Contrast Q J 10 9 8 7 6 with A K 6 5 4 3 2.

If you held the suit on the right, and partner had a singleton, you would always lose a trick or two to the opponents' middle cards. I do not mind seeing the opponents win tricks with aces and kings, but I do hate to see them win tricks with lesser cards.

In addition, you can expect to win two tricks with your ace and king even if another suit becomes trump. Therefore, you are not as desperate to see this suit become trump as you were when you held the Q J 10 9 8 7 6.

After your RHO has dealt and passed, don't preempt with a questionable hand.

Everyone knows to preempt aggressively in third seat (after two passes). It is equally clear that fourth seat is totally different — there's no reason to make a pushy preempt. However, many players don't realize: **preempting in first and second seat is not the same.**

The best time to preempt is when the opponents have the balance of power. As dealer with a weak hand and a long suit, there are three players who might have good hands. Because one is a friend and two are foes, the odds are 2:1 that the hand "belongs" to the other side. Therefore, bid 'em up.

However, when your RHO was unable to open, the odds change considerably. Only two players might have good hands — LHO and your partner. It is now "even money" as to which side is stronger.

Accordingly, the bottom line is:
Don't preempt in second seat with a marginal hand.

With both sides vulnerable, what would you do?
A. as dealer   B. after RHO passes

♠ A J 10 6 5 4 3   ♡ Q J 5   ◇ J 7   ♣ 8

A. Open 3♠. Not a classic hand, but you do have a seven-card suit and are eager to strike the first blow.

B. Pass. Too many flaws. Your suit is not great — you could easily lose two (or even three) trump tricks. Your ♠A and three outside honors give you a lot more defense than you'd like for a preempt. Because you have the highest-ranking suit, you should have no problem coming in later.

♠ 6 5   ♡ K Q 10 8 4 2   ◇ 8 7 2   ♣ 8 5

A. Open 2♡. They have the good cards. Don't let them have a free run.

B. Pass. You have only 5 HCP, no singleton, and you are vulnerable. Too many imperfections for a preempt in second seat.

No Majors? No Problem!

When you're short in both majors, it's a great time to preempt.

Everyone agrees that there are three desirable game contracts: 3NT, 4♡, and 4♠. When you don't have either major, the opponents probably have a fit in one or both of them. If they also have most of the HCP, they will do very well if left alone.

In fact, it's fair to say that weak hands with short majors call for desperate measures. Therefore, you should not only be eager to preempt, but whenever possible, look to "up the ante" by bidding "one more."

As dealer with neither side vulnerable:

♠ 7 6   ♡ 4   ♢ Q J 10 9 8 2   ♣ Q 9 5 3
Open 3♢. No majors, no defense, and "solid" trumps. Opening 2♢ is better than nothing, but is being too nice to the enemy. As for "Pass," for once, I'm speechless.

♠ 5   ♡ 3 2   ♢ 8 7 5 3   ♣ K J 10 8 6 4
Open 3♣. Some players complain about bad cards and pass a lot. Others prefer to bid (and win). The choice is yours.

FILLING THE VOID

If your only strength is in your long, strong suit — it's okay to preempt with a void.

When you're not confident which suit you belong in, you should think twice about preempting. However, when your long suit is strong and your other suits are not, it's definitely time to bid.

As dealer, regardless of vulnerability:

♠ A Q J 9 7 5 ♡ 9 6 3 ◇ — ♣ 8 5 4 2   Open 2♠

♠ — ♡ A K J 8 6 2 ◇ 5 4 2 ♣ 6 4 3 2   Open 2♡

♠ 8 5 3 ♡ 7 4 2 ◇ K Q 9 8 7 5 3 ♣ —   Open 3◇

♠ 9 6 3 ♡ — ◇ 8 4 2 ♣ A Q 8 7 4 3 2   Open 3♣

However, with these hands, a preempt is not warranted. Therefore, as dealer, regardless of vulnerability:

♠ 10 9 6 ♡ K 9 8 7 ◇ K Q 7 4 3 2 ♣ —   Pass

♠ A Q 7 5 4 2 ♡ Q 10 8 6 ◇ — ♣ 9 8 7   Pass

When partner opens a preempt, "support with support."

This is true regardless of your point count! In fact, the weaker you are, the harder you should try to "sock it to 'em." You already know that partner has a weak hand. If you're also weak, you don't want the opposition to have a free ride with their good cards.

"Support with support" also applies when vulnerable. Too many players are afraid — "I couldn't bid, I was vulnerable." However, they are overreacting.

Partner needs a better hand to make a vulnerable preempt. In effect, when he "dared" to preempt vulnerable despite his weak hand, he has already done the worrying for both of you. You can count on partner to have a better preempt, so don't be afraid.

How frisky can you be? The key is The Law (of Total Tricks). You are safe in bidding to the level equal to your number of trumps. When your side has nine trumps, don't hesitate bidding to the nine-trick (three) level. With 10 trumps, it's okay to bid to the four level.

West	*North*	*East*	*South*
—	2♡	Pass	???

Regardless of vulnerability, what would you do on each of the following?

♠ J 6 4   ♡ Q 3 2   ◇ K 8 6 5   ♣ 7 4 2

Bid 3♡. Lousy hand, lousy distribution. It's all irrelevant. All that matters is that your side has nine hearts, so you should be delighted to compete to the nine-trick level. Sometimes, bridge is an easy game.

♠ 9 3   ♡ K 8 4 2   ◇ A 5   ♣ 10 9 8 3 2

Bid 4♡. You don't expect to make it, but E-W are huge favorites to make 4♠. You are perfectly willing to table this dummy in 4♡ doubled. In fact, if partner's weak two-bid looks something like this:

♠ 8 7 5   ♡ A J 10 9 7 5   ◇ K 8 3   ♣ 5

he'll easily make 10 tricks.

By the way: You should make the same bids even if East had bid or doubled.

ONLY A SMALL TARGET

After partner opens 2♡ or 2♠, don't respond 2NT too often.

Once your partner preempts in a major suit, most very strong hands should jump to game in opener's major. With these hands, you rarely belong in 3NT or slam.

If your hand is not so wonderful, consider passing. Not only does partner have less than an opening bid, he usually has a lot less. Too many players respond 2NT with hands that are really going nowhere.

Responder should bid 2NT ONLY when he has:

> a blockbuster hand that is interested in slam

OR

> a borderline hand that may not make a game.

In both cases, responder is bidding 2NT to learn if opener has more than a minimum weak two-bid.

Partner deals and opens 2♡ (neither side vulnerable).

♠ A 5   ♡ A 9   ◇ A 9 8 5 3   ♣ A 6 4 3
Bid 4♡. No reason to bid 2NT. Regardless of what
partner has, this will be a great dummy in 4♡.

♠ A J 7 5   ♡ 3   ◇ K Q 7 4   ♣ K Q 6 3
Pass. You can't expect to make 3NT on your own.
Your singleton heart is a huge liability.

♠ A 5 4   ♡ 9 3   ◇ K Q 3 2   ♣ A Q 9 4
Bid 2NT. If partner shows a minimum by bidding 3♡,
you will pass. Otherwise, you'll bid 4♡. Even if
partner has the ♠K, you don't belong in 3NT.

♠ A Q J   ♡ K Q 7 5 3   ◇ K Q J   ♣ Q 9
Bid 4♡. Despite your 20 HCP, you shouldn't bother
looking for slam. Even if partner had both red aces
AND a singleton club, you'd still need the spade
finesse. Forget about it.

TO FORCE OR NOT TO FORCE

When partner preempts, every partnership must decide whether a new suit is forcing.

I recommend that you have the identical agreement every time you bid a new suit after partner preempts. That's a lot easier than trying to figure out the best approach on a case-by-case basis.

Some pairs vary their rules based on vulnerability, or whether the new suit is a major as opposed to a minor. While I understand the logic behind these points of view, I believe that those players are being impractical. Everyone already has so many conventions and agreements to remember — don't overload your memory. K.I.S.S. has always worked well for me.

My two cents: Many experienced players prefer "forcing," but I strongly prefer "nonforcing" — why force partner to bid again when he's already told his story?

Here are some examples of "new suit after preempt" auctions. In each case, partner preempted and you responded 3♢. In your partnership, is 3♢ forcing?

West	Partner	East	You
1♡	2♠	Pass	3♢
1♡	2♠	Dbl	3♢
1♡	2♠	3♣	3♢
—	2♠	Pass	3♢
Pass	2♠	Dbl	3♢
—	2♠	3♣	3♢
Pass	3♣	Pass	3♢
—	3♣	Dbl	3♢

In my partnership with Larry Cohen, the 3♢ bid was always nonforcing. We wanted to be able to bid 3♢ with a hand such as:

♠ 4   ♡ 8 7 5 4   ♢ A K J 10 8 6 3   ♣ A

without demanding that the preemptor bid again.

DESPERATE MEASURES NEEDED

Once partner passes, RHO opens, and your hand is weak and shapely, "bid 'em up!"

If you're weak, and partner couldn't open, the opponents probably have a game. After two passes, you would try to preempt aggressively or open light. Don't alter your approach just because RHO opened.

Partner passes and your RHO opens 1♣.
The opponents are vulnerable, you are not.

♠ A K J 9   ♡ 6   ◇ 8 7 5   ♣ 10 8 7 4 3
Bid 1♠. Make it tougher for them to find a heart fit and/or exchange information. Make it easy for partner to find the best lead.

♠ 6   ♡ Q J 10 8 7   ◇ 9 4 3 2   ♣ 9 6 5
Bid 2♡. With 3 HCP opposite a passed hand, you are positive that the opponents can make a game (or slam). You may not be able to stop them, but you can certainly make them work harder to get there.

By the way: If the vulnerability is less attractive, it's okay to be discreet.

Chapter 8

Cue-Bids:
Unravel the Mystery

THE STAYMAN REPLACEMENT

When partner opens 1NT and RHO makes a natural overcall, your cue-bid serves as Stayman.

The "Stayman cue-bid" is game-forcing, promising 10+ HCP and four cards in an unbid major.

West	North	East	South
Pass	1NT	2♠	???

♠ 7 5　♡ K 7 6 4　♢ A Q J 2　♣ J 6 3
Cue-bid 3♠. This says nothing about your spades.

♠ 7 5　♡ K 7 6　♢ A Q J 2　♣ J 6 3 2
Bid 3NT. You need four hearts to bid Stayman here. Don't worry; partner probably has a spade stopper.

♠ 4　♡ 9 5　♢ J 8 5 3　♣ Q J 10 6 4 2
Bid 3♣. This is NOT Stayman, you're just competing. Partner must pass. With a stronger hand, you would jump to 3NT.

By the way: If RHO's overcall is artificial, all bets are off. Many approaches are possible, so each pair must decide what to do.

When an opponent bids one suit and 3NT is possible, a three-level cue-bid ASKS. This is referred to as a Western Cue-Bid.

After the enemy bids a suit, you can bid 3NT with a stopper in his suit and a suitable hand. A cue-bid is necessary when you lack a stopper, and you want to ask partner if he has one. Don't be nervous about other suits — you can't afford to worry about sneak attacks.

West	North	East	South
—	—	1♥	2♦
Pass	3♦	Pass	???

♠ A Q ♡ 6 4 ◇ A J 9 7 5 4 3 ♣ K 4
Cue-bid 3♡. If partner has a heart stopper, 3NT is looking good. If partner can't oblige, you will decide whether to play 5◇ or stop in 4◇.

♠ K 7 ♡ K Q 9 ◇ A K 10 7 6 4 ♣ 7 5
Bid 3NT. You can't be concerned about clubs.

♠ A J 9 7 ♡ 9 6 ◇ A Q 10 9 5 2 ♣ A
Bid 3♠. If partner has four spades, you want to play in spades. Partner can still bid 3NT with a heart stopper.

A TELL - TALE SIGN

When the opponents bid two suits and 3NT is possible, a three-level cue-bid TELLS.

With two suits in the picture, your perspective changes. If you're interested in 3NT and have one of their suits stopped, you bid that suit. If partner has a stopper in their other suit, he will bid notrump. If he doesn't have a stopper, he will retreat.

West	North	East	South
West	*North*	*East*	*South*
1♡	Pass	1♠	2♢
Pass	3♢	Pass	???

♠ A Q ♡ 6 4 ♢ A J 9 7 5 4 3 ♣ K 4
Cue-bid 3♠. You have spades stopped, but not hearts.

♠ K 7 ♡ K Q 9 ♢ A K 10 7 6 4 ♣ 7 5
Bid 3NT. You have stoppers in both of their suits.

♠ 9 6 ♡ A J 9 7 ♢ A Q 10 9 5 2 ♣ A
Cue-bid 3♡. Strong hearts, weak spades.

Memory aid: Note the two "T" words.
"If the enemy bids **Two** suits, a cue-bid **Tells**."

HAPPY TOGETHER

When partner opens and RHO overcalls, a cue-bid promises support for opener's suit.

Question 1: Is this true for both majors and minors?
Answer: YES. In addition, if partner opened 1♣ or 1♢, responder's cue-bid denies four cards in an unbid major.

Question 2: How strong must responder be?
Answer: Some partnerships require an opening bid; now the auction is game-forcing. Others treat the cue-bid as a "limit raise or better," which is not forcing to game. Clearly, a meeting of the minds is required.

Question 3: How much support does responder need?
Answer: If partner opens in a major, three cards is okay. If partner opens in a minor, you would like to have five-card support, but you may have to make do with only four.

Question 4: Does the cue-bid say anything about your holding in the opponent's suit?
Answer: No.

West	North	East	South
Pass	1♢	1♠	???

♠ A 5 3   ♡ K 8   ♢ A 9 8 7 2   ♣ Q 10 6

Cue-bid 2♠. You may belong in 3NT, but for now, tell partner about your nice diamonds and good hand.

♠ 8 6   ♡ A J 10   ♢ K Q 6 4 2   ♣ 7 5 3

If 3♢ shows a limit raise here, that's perfect.
If 3♢ would be weak in competition, cue-bid 2♠.

♠ 8 7   ♡ K J 5 3   ♢ A K Q 7 3   ♣ 6 2

Gorgeous diamonds! Sorry, but they'll have to wait.
Show your major first by making a negative double.

West	North	East	South
—	1♡	2♢	???

♠ A K   ♡ 4 3 2   ♢ A 5 4 3   ♣ A J 5 3

Cue-bid 3♢. I've seen better heart support. However, with your big hand, the best way to investigate the possibility of slam is to support partner ASAP.

When partner makes a negative double, opener's cue-bid is forcing to game. Any distribution is possible.

West	North	East	South
—	—	Pass	1♢
1♠	Dbl	Pass	???

North's double showed 6+ points and 4+ hearts. South should cue-bid 2♠ with each hand below.

♠ A   ♡ K J 6   ♢ A K J 9 2   ♣ A 9 5 3
This hand might belong in hearts, diamonds, clubs, or notrump. You want to tell partner that you're strong enough to insist on game (at least), and that you need information from him.

♠ 8 5 3   ♡ A 2   ♢ A K Q J 8 7   ♣ A 6
Too strong to jump to 3♢, which partner could pass.

♠ 3   ♡ A Q 10 4   ♢ K Q J 8 3   ♣ A K 5
You know that you belong in hearts, but an immediate jump to 4♡ might miss a slam.

Note how East – West communicated to reach their optimum contract.

West			*East*
♠ 8			♠ 7 5 4
♡ A Q 7			♡ K J 10 8
◇ A Q 6 3			◇ 7 4 2
♣ A K 9 3 2			♣ Q J 5

West	*North*	*East*	*South*
1♣	1♠	Dbl	Pass
2♠	Pass	3♣	Pass
3◇	Pass	3♡	Pass
4♡	All Pass		

Once East promised some values with his double, West cue-bid 2♠ to force to game. East couldn't bid notrump without a spade stopper, so he took a preference to opener's first suit.

West bid 3◇ to show his second suit. East had already promised four hearts with the negative double, but he appreciated his three heart honors. He bid 3♡ to emphasize the *quality* of that suit. West was now happy to raise to 4♡, which made easily.

THE NON CUE - BID

After your opponent's artificial bid, if you bid that same suit, it is NOT a cue-bid, it is a natural overcall.

Many players regard the subject of cue-bids as strange and mysterious. This is especially true when your opponent has not promised the suit he bid. Remember, **You can cue-bid the suit bid by your opponent only when his bid guaranteed that suit.**

On the auctions below, South's bid shows a great suit. With a not-so-great suit, he would content himself with a lead-directing double.

West	North	East	South
—	—	2♣	3♣

East's artificial 2♣ bid promised a great hand, and said nothing about clubs. South's bid shows a long, strong club suit. He is hoping to make life difficult for E-W.

West	North	East	South
2♣	Pass	2◇	3◇

Everyone agrees that 2◇ does not show diamonds, so the 3◇ bid is natural.

West	North	East	South
1NT	Pass	2♣	3♣

East's Stayman bid was artificial. South had a great club suit.

West	North	East	South
1NT	Pass	2◇*	3◇
	*transfer to hearts		

East promised hearts. 3◇ shows gorgeous diamonds.

By the way: When an opponent's artificial bid guarantees a specific (other) suit, you *can* make a cue-bid by bidding the suit he actually promised.

West	North	East	South
1NT	Pass	2◇*	2♡
	*transfer to hearts		

2♡ IS a cue-bid. South is showing spades and a minor (Michaels), just as if East opened 1♡.

After partner's Michaels Cue-Bid, a jump raise in his major promises good support, not "points."

Remember, you need to choose one of partner's two five-card suits, even if you hate both of them. When you really do like his suit, tell him the good news by jumping. This illustrates "support with support," "points schmoints," and The LAW of Total Tricks.

West	North	East	South
West	*North*	*East*	*South*
1♣	2♣	Pass	???

♠ K Q 9 5   ♡ 7 6   ◇ J 8 6 2   ♣ Q 7 2
Jump to 3♠ to tell partner that you have **a great fit** for spades. With your nine-card fit (his 5 + your 4), you are delighted to be at the nine-trick level.

♠ J 7   ♡ 4   ◇ K 7 5 3 2   ♣ K J 7 4 3
Bid 2♠. You **prefer spades to hearts,** nothing more.

♠ K 9 7 6 4   ♡ J 6   ◇ A 2   ♣ 9 8 5 4
Jump to 4♠ (5+5=10). Even if you don't make it, this will be a cheap sacrifice.

Chapter 9

Overcalls –
Yes, No, Maybe

A jump-overcall in the balancing seat shows a good hand. It is not a Weak Jump Overcall (WJO).

This is "standard bridge." The logic here is that you don't have to "waste your time" preempting once an opponent has announced that he is broke. Therefore, the jump is intermediate, promising VOB, as opposed to a weak hand that was "just balancing."

West	*North*	*East*	*South*
1♢	Pass	Pass	???

♠ J 5 2   ♡ K Q J 8 6 5   ♢ 3   ♣ A J 10
Bid 2♡. A classic jump-overcall in the balancing seat.

♠ J 5 2   ♡ K Q J 8 6 5   ♢ 3   ♣ 6 5 4
Bid 1♡. You lack the values needed to jump to 2♡ in the balancing seat. Yes, you would have preempted if your RHO had opened — but he didn't.

♠ A J 2   ♡ K Q J 8 6 5   ♢ 3   ♣ A J 10
Double. With this very nice hand, you are too strong to jump to 2♡.

NOT HIS STRONG SUIT

If you have a good hand, it's okay to overcall at the one level with a lousy five-card suit.

Obviously, everyone would prefer to have a strong suit. However, you can't wait for perfect hands. If the hand is promising, and a takeout double is out of the question, bid now rather than guess later.

West	North	East	South
—	—	1♣	???

♠ A K 4   ♡ 4   ◊ Q 8 7 5 3   ♣ A 7 5 3
Overcall 1◊.

♠ A   ♡ 10 7 6 3 2   ◊ A K J   ♣ Q 7 6 4
Overcall 1♡.

♠ J 9 7 5 4   ♡ 8   ◊ A K 8 3   ♣ A 7 4
Overcall 1♠.

An overcall at the 2+ level usually includes VOB. However, never say never.

West	North	East	South
—	—	1♠	???

♠ 9 4 ♡ 7 4 ◇ A K Q 10 6 5 4 ♣ 5 3
Overcall 2◇. Don't preempt with seven solid tricks.

West	North	East	South
—	—	2◇	???

♠ K 6 5 ♡ K Q J 10 4 2 ◇ 3 ♣ 7 6 4
Overcall 2♡. A jump to 3♡ is out — that would show a big hand (you can't preempt a preempt). You wouldn't pass, would you?

West	North	East	South
—	—	4♡	???

♠ A K 10 9 7 6 5 4 ♡ 8 ◇ 8 3 2 ♣ 4
Overcall 4♠, obviously.

Up, Up, and Away

The higher the level of RHO's initial action, the better your hand must be in order to bid or double.

Evaluating how strong your hand needs to be goes a lot further than counting HCP. Your distribution is very important. Remember: **the shorter you are in the opponent's suit, the harder you try to take action.**

When you make a takeout double at a high level, you are forcing partner to bid. If you do so with a mediocre hand, you will place him in a no-win situation.

After a questionable double, if partner has:

- a weak hand, he will go down, perhaps doubled
- 10 points, he will jump and again be too high
- a terrific hand, he will bid slam and go down

If all you have is a "dubious double," you should pass. If partner does have a worthwhile hand, he is welcome to balance.

With neither side vulnerable, what would you do if:
  A: RHO opens 1♣   B: RHO opens 3♣

♠ Q 8 6 5   ♡ A Q J   ◇ J 6 4 3   ♣ K 6

A: Double. This is automatic. Even if partner is very weak, you are not in trouble at the one level.

B: Pass. You certainly don't want to force partner to bid at the three level when he might be broke.

♠ 5   ♡ A Q J 9 8   ◇ K 6 3   ♣ J 8 5 2

A: Overcall 1♡. This is beyond obvious.

B: Pass. Despite the great suit, you have no business being at the three level on your own. Your length in the opponent's suit is an offensive liability.

♠ 10 8 6 5   ♡ A Q 9   ◇ A J 10 7 6   ♣ 3

A: Double. Far more flexible than a 1◇ overcall.

B: Double. Points schmoints! The singleton in the opponent's suit says, "go for it."

If you'd like to bid after an opponent's three-level preempt, think 3NT.

Although 4♡ and 4♠ are usually the most desirable game contracts, once an opponent shows a seven-card suit, you should reconsider. 3NT is now the #1 priority. Why is that?

Because one opponent has a long suit and several short suits, you have good reason to be concerned about ruffs and bad trump splits. These would be a big problem in a suit contract — but notrump is a different story. If you're concerned about their long suit in notrump, not to worry. It's very unlikely that the preemptor will ever get in to run his long suit. **Entryless defenders are harmless in notrump.**

A 3NT overcall includes a VERY WIDE range of HCP and distribution. With a balanced hand, 16 HCP is the usual minimum, while the maximum is a lot higher.

It is comforting to have two stoppers, but one is okay. Ax or Axx is the most desirable single stopper because a holdup play will cut the opponents' communication.

West	North	East	South
—	—	3♡	???

♠ Q 8 4 2   ♡ A 9   ◇ A K J   ♣ K Q 5 2
Bid 3NT. You might belong in spades, but if partner
holds ♠ K 6 5 3, you could have three trump losers.
You have no such worry in notrump. If you double
and partner bids 4♣ or 4◇, you are not well-placed.

♠ K 6   ♡ A 8 5   ◇ A K Q J 8 4   ♣ J 2
Bid 3NT. Definitely gorgeous diamonds, but the time
to talk about them is when they're on your finger.
Picture partner with just the ♠A, and decide where
you'd like to play after a heart lead.

♠ K 9 3   ♡ K J 5   ◇ J   ♣ A K J 9 5 2
Bid 3NT. Many players would be afraid to overcall
3NT with a singleton. However, bidding 4♣ would
represent "scared bridge." The opponents will not
know that you have only one diamond. Your chances
of making 3NT are infinitely better than making 5♣.

♠ Q J   ♡ A K 6   ◇ K J 6 4   ♣ A K Q J
Bid 3NT. You don't like making the same bid with
24 HCP as you did with 16, but what's the alternative?

LOOK MA, NO STOPPER

You don't need a stopper in opener's suit to balance with 1NT.

Because you are reluctant to sell out at the one level, all you need is 10-14 HCP. Once your RHO passed the opening bid, you know partner must have some values. He'll often have good cards in their suit. If you don't have a suit to bid, or the right shape to double, a stopperless 1NT is your only alternative to a pass.

Here are some hands where you should balance with 1NT despite not having a stopper in opener's suit.

By the way: As a passed hand, you would only need 9-11 HCP to balance with 1NT.

West	North	East	South
West	*North*	*East*	*South*
1♣	Pass	Pass	???

Bid 1NT with both:

♠ A J 10   ♡ K 7   ◇ K J 5 3   ♣ 6 4 3 2

♠ A 2   ♡ Q J 4 3   ◇ A 10 4 2   ♣ J 7 5

West	North	East	South
1◇	Pass	Pass	???

Bid 1NT with both:

♠ K 6 5 2 ♡ Q 2 ◇ 10 6 4 ♣ A K J 9

♠ A 4 ♡ A Q 10 ◇ 9 8 4 ♣ J 7 6 4 3

West	North	East	South
1♡	Pass	Pass	???

Bid 1NT with both:

♠ K 4 ♡ 8 7 4 2 ◇ K Q 9 4 ♣ A 7 3

♠ 7 4 ♡ 9 7 2 ◇ A J 10 8 ♣ A Q 9 2

West	North	East	South
1♠	Pass	Pass	???

Bid 1NT with both:

♠ 8 4 3 2 ♡ K 5 ◇ A Q 9 ♣ K J 8 4

♠ J 9 4 ♡ 9 2 ◇ A K 8 7 ♣ A 10 6 2

DON'T FORCE THE ISSUE

After partner overcalls at the one level, a new suit should not be forcing.

I don't recommend that a new suit be forcing, even by an unpassed hand. The opening bidder has promised VOB, while partner has not. After an auction such as:

West	North	East	South
1♢	1♠	Pass	???

♠ 4   ♡ K Q 10 7 3 2   ♢ 8 4 3   ♣ A 5 2

I'd like to bid 2♡ and show my nice suit without forcing North to bid again when all he has is a minimum overcall. If partner has something to say, he is welcome to do so.

♠ A 4   ♡ K Q 10 7 3 2   ♢ A 8 3   ♣ A 5

Cue-bid 2♢. You have such a great hand that you can't risk partner's passing a 2♡ response. If partner rebids 2♠, you'll bid 3♡, which is 100% forcing.

Chapter 10

I'll Have
a Double

WHO NEEDS A FOURTH?

Although you prefer to have four cards in the unbid major for a takeout double, sometimes you have only three.

Players who refuse to make takeout doubles with fewer than four cards in the unbid major are impractical perfectionists.

West	North	East	South
—	—	1♠	???

♠ 5 4　♡ K 8 4　◇ A K 7 5　♣ A J 9 6

You should not consider any action other than double. If partner responds 2♡ and has to play in a 4-3 fit at the two level, the world will *not* end.

♠ 5　♡ A J 9　◇ A Q 8 6　♣ Q 7 5 3 2

If you would pass or overcall, I will agree that you are entitled to your (wrong) opinion. As for myself, I would double and wonder, "What's the problem?" The flexible takeout double is the standout action.

IT DOESN'T TAKE MUCH

If your RHO bids after partner's takeout double, you don't need a lot to compete.

Everyone knows that you are off the hook after RHO bids. Therefore, many players overreact, and pass unless they have solid values. no, No, NO!

Once partner promised a reasonable hand with the unbid suits, all you need is something worth saying.

West	North	East	South
1♣	Dbl	1♠	???

♠ 9 8 5 ♡ Q J 7 3 ◇ A 8 ♣ 8 7 4 3
Bid 2♡. Why not show your major? A four-card suit is not a problem.

♠ 7 4 ♡ J 4 2 ◇ K Q 10 6 ♣ 9 6 3 2
Bid 2◇. If West becomes declarer, you desperately want a diamond lead.

♠ A ♡ K J 9 6 4 ◇ 8 6 4 3 ♣ 7 5 2
Bid 3♡. With this hand, you owe partner a jump.

East had only 3 HCP, but his spades were attractive.

Contract: 3NT
Lead: ♠2

North
♠ Q 5
♡ 10 4
♢ K Q 10 7 3
♣ 10 6 4 2

West
♠ J 4 3 2
♡ K Q 9 8
♢ 4
♣ K Q 9 7

East
♠ K 10 9 8 7
♡ 7 6 2
♢ 8 2
♣ 8 5 3

South
♠ A 6
♡ A J 5 3
♢ A J 9 6 5
♣ A J

West	North	East	South
—	Pass	Pass	1♢
Dbl	3♢	3♠	3NT
All Pass			

West would never have led a spade on his own, but he trusted his partner's bid. After the spade lead, South had no chance. Down one!

TELL ME MORE, TELL ME MORE

When the opponents bid and raise a suit, and partner has doubled or overcalled, your double is takeout.

Although the above seems obvious and logical, it is alertable. It's referred to as a Responsive Double.

Here is one example of this very useful convention. You are South, in the following auction:

West	North	East	South
1♡	Dbl	2♡	???

♠ A 6 3   ♡ 7 4   ◇ Q 6 4 2   ♣ K 7 5 3

After partner's takeout double, you want to compete. You certainly won't get rich defending 2♡. However, you have no idea what suit to bid. If you guess a minor, you may hit partner's three-card suit instead of a suit with four or even five cards.

The solution is to ask partner to make the decision. Your Responsive Double asks him to choose a suit. Because you didn't bid spades, he will usually bid a minor. However, if his spades look like ♠ K Q 10 9, he is welcome to bid that suit.

As long as the opponents bid *and* raise, Responsive
Doubles are also on after partner has overcalled.

West	North	East	South
1♠	2♣	2♠	???

♠ 6 3   ♡ A K 5 4   ◇ K 8 7 5 2   ♣ 8 6

Considering that everyone is bidding, you have a pretty
good hand. What suit should you bid? Who knows?
Once again, the flexible solution is to double.

By the way: How high should Responsive Doubles
be played? When your opponents have voluntarily bid
and raised to a high level, you are unlikely to have a
trump stack. Double should still be responsive when
the opposition bids game. Obviously, partner will pass
your double when he has nothing to bid.

West	North	East	South
3♠	4♡	4♠	???

South should double with each of these hands:

♠ 9 7   ♡ K 5   ◇ A K 9 6 3   ♣ K 8 7 6

♠ A 8   ♡ 5   ◇ K Q 9 8   ♣ Q J 7 5 4 2

♠ 6 4 2   ♡ 9 4   ◇ A Q 10   ♣ A J 9 6 3

Take It to the Max

You open a major, partner raises to two,
and RHO bids the suit directly under yours.
A double invites game, not penalties.

This alertable convention is necessary for opener
because bidding three of his major is not invitational.
It would just be a competitive bid based on a shapely,
minimum opening bid.

When opener has an invitational hand of 17-18 points
(including distribution), he needs a way to invite game.
If RHO bids the "one under" suit, a Maximal Overcall
Double is the only answer.

The two basic Maximal Overcall Double auctions are:

West	North	East	South
—	Pass	Pass	1♡
Pass	2♡	3◇	Dbl

West	North	East	South
—	—	—	1♠
Pass	2♠	3♡	Dbl

West	North	East	South
—	—	—	1♡
Pass	2♡	3◇	???

♠ K 8 5 4   ♡ A K J 10 3   ◇ 6   ♣ K 6 3

Double. Partner will jump to 4♡ with a maximum, sign off in 3♡ with a minimum, and pass with great diamonds. All non-penalty doubles give partner the option of passing for penalties with a suitable hand.

♠ K Q   ♡ K Q J 9 6 4   ◇ 5 4   ♣ Q 10 8

Bid 3♡, to play.

♠ A 8   ♡ A 7 6 4 2   ◇ K Q 10 5   ♣ 4 3

Pass. You would like to make a penalty double, but we are playing Maximal Overcall Doubles. Not to worry — these hands are rare.

♠ 9 8 4   ♡ A K 10 6 4 2   ◇ —   ♣ K Q J 8

Bid 4♡. You have enough offense to insist on game.

By the way: If West bids or doubles (instead of passing), nothing changes. As long as East bid the "one under" suit, South's double is maximal.

I, Who Have Nothing

If partner opens 2♣ and RHO overcalls, a double should show a lousy hand (0-3 HCP).

The double says nothing about your holding in the opponent's suit. It warns partner that he is on his own.

This convention has been well-received and easy to remember. Opponents are competing more these days, so you must be prepared.

West	North	East	South
—	2♣	2♡	???

♠ 8 6 4   ♡ J 5 3 2   ◇ 10 8 6 5   ♣ 9 2
Double. North now alerts. If asked, he will explain: "Shows 0-3 HCP. Says nothing about hearts."

♠ A 9 8   ♡ 9 6   ◇ K 6 5 4   ♣ 9 6 5 3
Pass. North now alerts. If asked, he will explain: "Promises at least 4 HCP. Forcing to game."

By the way: If RHO doubles, a redouble indicates the lousy hand.

By the way #2: Some players prefer to switch "pass" and "double," so that "pass" is weaker.

Chapter 11

Impressive
Declarer Play

When missing six cards in a suit, a 3-3 split is against the odds. Don't count on it.

Contract: 4♠
Lead: ♡J

North
♠ 10 6
♡ 7 5 4 2
♢ 6 5
♣ K 9 7 5 2

South
♠ A K 7 4 3
♡ 9
♢ A K Q J 10
♣ A 4

The defense began with two rounds of hearts. After ruffing the second, declarer cashed his ace and king of trumps. He now had two small spades. If the opponents' two remaining trumps divided 1-1, he could safely play a third round and score up an overtrick. However, if they split 2-0, as expected, playing a third round would enable the defense to draw trumps and run hearts. Instead, declarer simply ran diamonds and conceded two trump tricks, keeping control of the hand while guaranteeing 10 tricks.

When declaring in notrump, you don't always have the time to set up your best suit. Don't give up — look for alternatives.

Contract: 3NT
Lead: ♠Q

North
♠ A K
♡ 3 2
◇ 8 7 5 3
♣ Q J 10 8 2

South
♠ 8 6
♡ A K 10
◇ A K Q J
♣ 9 5 4 3

Declarer's thought process:
"Nice spades, partner, I was worried about that suit. I've got eight easy tricks: two spades, two hearts, and four diamonds. For my ninth trick, I'll just work on clubs. Wait a minute. Darn it, there's a problem. Before I can win any clubs, they'll set up their suit and win three spades and two clubs. 3NT is hopeless."

"Wait, there's still hope. If East has the queen and jack of hearts, I can finesse the ♡10 for my ninth trick. I'd better do it right now, while I'm on the board."

At trick two, lead a heart to your ten and hope.

North
♠ A K
♡ 3 2
♢ 8 7 5 3
♣ Q J 10 8 2

West
♠ Q J 10 7 5
♡ 9 7 6
♢ 10 6 2
♣ K 7

East
♠ 9 4 3 2
♡ Q J 8 5 4
♢ 9 4
♣ A 6

South
♠ 8 6
♡ A K 10
♢ A K Q J
♣ 9 5 4 3

When an opponent leads a suit, it is usually correct to duck with Axx opposite xx in suit contracts as well as notrump.

Everyone knows about holdup plays in notrump. However, **lose your losers early** also allows declarer to maintain control in a suit contract.

Contract: 4♡
Lead: ♠Q

North
♠ 7 3
♡ A K
♢ Q 7 6 5 3
♣ A 7 4 3

South
♠ A 8 2
♡ Q J 10 8 7 4 3
♢ J
♣ J 5

West	North	East	South
Pass	1♢	Pass	1♡
Pass	2♣	Pass	3♡
Pass	4♡	All Pass	

136

South's second-round jump to 3♡ was invitational.
With a better hand, he could have jumped to 4♡ or bid
Fourth Suit Game-Forcing (2♠). North was delighted
to accept the invitation, based on the quality of his
heart support.

South needed to ruff a spade in dummy for his tenth
trick. With only one quick entry to his hand, he ducked
the opening lead. West shifted to a trump, hoping to
stop a spade ruff, but declarer was in control. South
led a spade to his ace and ruffed a spade on the board.
Declarer lost only three tricks — one spade, one
diamond, and one club.

If South made the mistake of winning the first spade
and conceding a spade, he would be in trouble. The
defenders would shift to a trump. When declarer then
led a minor suit from the board, the defense would win
and lead a second trump. Now declarer was destined
to lose a second spade trick and be down one.

With an "iffy" suit, draw trumps and strip
both your hands of any irrelevant suit.
Now, throw the enemy in with a sure loser.

Contract: 4♠
Lead: ♢K

North
♠ K J 9 8
♡ J 6 5
♢ 9 8
♣ A J 6 4

South
♠ A Q 10 7 6 5 2
♡ Q 7 4
♢ A 2
♣ 9

South was willing to lose one diamond trick and two
hearts. However, if he led hearts, he rated to lose a
third heart trick after both heart honors were captured.

Declarer needed to throw the opponents in with his
diamond loser and force them to lead hearts. But —
first things first. Before doing so, South had to get rid
of *all* of dummy's clubs.

Declarer won the diamond lead with his ace and led
a club to dummy's ace. South ruffed a club with his
♠10, and led a trump to dummy's eight. Declarer
ruffed another club with his ♠5, and led a spade to
the nine. He then ruffed dummy's last club.

N-S won the first seven tricks, which left:

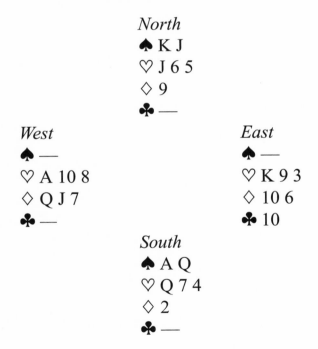

North
♠ K J
♡ J 6 5
◇ 9
♣ —

West
♠ —
♡ A 10 8
◇ Q J 7
♣ —

East
♠ —
♡ K 9 3
◇ 10 6
♣ 10

South
♠ A Q
♡ Q 7 4
◇ 2
♣ —

Declarer led the ◇2 and claimed. No matter what was
led, South would lose only two heart tricks.

I'm Behind You All the Way

Leading from weakness toward strength can be crucial even if there is no finesse.

If you're afraid that a defender might be void in a particular suit, don't give that opponent the chance to ruff a WINNER.

Contract: 4♠
Lead: ♡A

North
♠ A J 3
♡ 8 6 2
♢ K 8 7 2
♣ 7 6 4

South
♠ K Q 10 8 7 5
♡ J 10
♢ —
♣ A K 8 5 3

West	North	East	South
—	—	—	1♠
Dbl	2♠	Pass	4♠
All Pass			

West led hearts, and continued the suit. South ruffed the third round and turned his attention to clubs. West had promised length with his takeout double. If West had only three clubs, all was well. If he had all five, no chance. Therefore, South focused on a 4-1 club split.

He cashed the ♣A and led a spade to the ace. He then led a club from dummy. East was fixed. If he ruffed, South would pull East's last trump and ruff out West's clubs. If East discarded, declarer would win the ♣K, concede a club, and eventually ruff a club with the ♠J.

Contract: 4♠
Lead: ♡A

North
♠ A J 3
♡ 8 6 2
◇ K 8 7 2
♣ 7 6 4

West
♠ 2
♡ A K 9 4
◇ A Q 10 9
♣ Q 10 9 2

East
♠ 9 6 4
♡ Q 7 5 3
◇ J 6 5 4 3
♣ J

South
♠ K Q 10 8 7 5
♡ J 10
◇ —
♣ A K 8 5 3

When declarer has a choice of where to win a trick, think carefully about where you'll need to be **later on**.

	North	
Contract: 3NT	♠ A 9 7 5 4	
Lead: ♡J	♡ K 7 4	
	◇ A K 10	
	♣ A 4	

West		*East*
♠ K 10		♠ Q J 8 3
♡ J 10 9 5 2		♡ Q 8 6
◇ J 7 5		◇ Q 9 2
♣ 8 7 5		♣ K 6 3

	South	
	♠ 6 2	
	♡ A 3	
	◇ 8 6 4 3	
	♣ Q J 10 9 2	

West	*North*	*East*	*South*
Pass	1♠	Pass	1NT
Pass	3NT	All Pass	

Declarer has six sure winners in aces and kings: one spade, two hearts, two diamonds and one club. He needs three additional tricks, and clubs are obviously the best suit to develop.

Don't make the mistake of winning the ♡A and leading the ♣Q (which would also block the suit). South is guaranteed to win three extra tricks in clubs as long as he can get to his hand *after* the clubs are established. He must save his ♡A for later.

Instead, South should win the opening lead with dummy's ♡K and play the ♣A, and then continue with the ♣4. The opponents can win their ♣K whenever they choose, but declarer is sitting pretty with his club winners and carefully-preserved ♡A.

The recommended way to play a suit may not be the best way to play the hand.

Contract: 6♡
Lead: ♢J

North
♠ A Q 7 5 3 2
♡ 10 8
♢ 7 6
♣ 8 5 4

South
♠ K 8
♡ A K J 9 7 6
♢ A Q
♣ A K 3

Everyone knows to finesse with a total of eight cards missing the queen. However, crossing to dummy in spades to take the heart finesse would block the spade suit and risk a ruff. Instead, lay down the ace and king of hearts. If the ♡Q does not fall, continue hearts until they take their winner. Even if one player started with four hearts to the queen, no problem. You'll draw all his trumps, cash your spades, and discard the ♣3.

Chapter 12

The Defense Never Rests

When a defender knows that HE must get the lead, he's gotta do what he's gotta do.

	North	
Contract: 4♡	♠ 8	
Lead: ♠K	♡ A K J 4	
	◇ A K Q J 8	
	♣ 8 4 3	

West		*East*
♠ K Q 10 6 2		♠ A 9 7 5
♡ 8 7		♡ 3 2
◇ 6 5 4		◇ 9 7 2
♣ A 10 9		♣ Q J 6 2

	South	
	♠ J 4 3	
	♡ Q 10 9 6 5	
	◇ 10 3	
	♣ K 7 5	

A very imposing dummy! If East would like to defeat 4♡, he had better make his move NOW, and overtake West's ♠K with his ♠A, so he can lead the ♣Q. This allows the defense to take the first four tricks. If East ducks the ♠K, South's ♣K is well-protected from an attack by West.

Respect partner's signals. He knows more about his hand than you do.

North (dummy)

Contract: 4♠

Lead: ◇Q

♠ —
♡ A K Q
◇ K 8 6 5 3
♣ A 10 5 3 2

West (you)
♠ 9
♡ J 9 8 5 2
◇ Q J
♣ Q 9 8 6 4

West	North	East	South
Pass	1◇	Pass	4♠
All Pass			

Despite North's bid, you elect to lead the ◇Q. Things are looking up when you win the first trick, as partner plays the ◇2 and South the ◇7. You are all set to lead the ◇J, but pause to reflect. What is going on? Why was partner screaming, "I hate diamonds," when he must have the ◇A? What should you lead now?

Here is the entire hand:

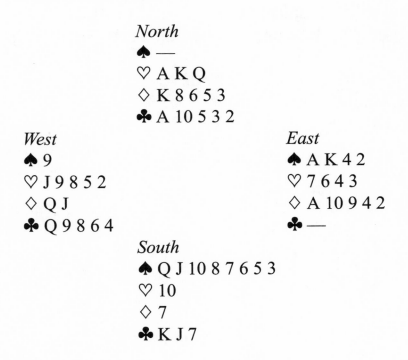

North
♠ —
♡ A K Q
♢ K 8 6 5 3
♣ A 10 5 3 2

West
♠ 9
♡ J 9 8 5 2
♢ Q J
♣ Q 9 8 6 4

East
♠ A K 4 2
♡ 7 6 4 3
♢ A 10 9 4 2
♣ —

South
♠ Q J 10 8 7 6 5 3
♡ 10
♢ 7
♣ K J 7

Did you get partner's message and find the essential club shift? If you don't give partner a club ruff, South will draw trumps and lose only one diamond and two spade tricks.

If declarer is drawing trumps, a defender should (usually) take his ace of trumps when he has only one small card remaining.

Contract: 4♡
Lead: ◇K

North
♠ A K J 3
♡ 10 7 5
◇ 8 6 5
♣ 10 7 4

West
♠ 10 7 2
♡ A 6 4 3
◇ K Q J 3
♣ 8 3

East
♠ Q 9 6 5 4
♡ 2
◇ A 9 7 4
♣ 6 5 2

South
♠ 8
♡ K Q J 9 8
◇ 10 2
♣ A K Q J 9

West	North	East	South
—	—	—	1♡
Pass	2♡	Pass	4♡
All Pass			

150

The defense led diamonds, and declarer ruffed the third round. With no problems in the other suits, he began drawing trumps. If West won the first or second round of hearts, declarer could easily draw trumps and run his clubs. However, when West ducked twice (waiting until he held the ♡A 6), the contract was doomed.

If declarer led a third trump, West would win and lead a diamond. This would force out declarer's last trump, and West would win his ♡6.

Instead, declarer abandoned trumps, and cashed the ♠A. He then played clubs, hoping that West would follow to three rounds. If he did, South could continue clubs, and West's ♡6 would never win a trick, because North could overruff.

Unfortunately, West ruffed the third club with the ♡6 and cashed the ♡A. Down one, a nice reward for defensive patience.

Say No to Second - Hand Low

When your partner's opening lead against a notrump contract seems promising, try to preserve HIS entries.

Contract: 3NT
Lead: ♡Q

North
♠ A 10 8
♡ A K
◇ Q J 10 9 7
♣ A 10 7

West
♠ J 7 5 4
♡ Q J 10 6 4 3
◇ K 3
♣ J

East
♠ Q 9 2
♡ 9 7
◇ A 5 4 2
♣ Q 9 5 3

South
♠ K 6 3
♡ 8 5 2
◇ 8 6
♣ K 8 6 4 2

West	North	East	South
—	1◇	Pass	1NT
Pass	3NT	All Pass	

East realized that his only hope of defeating the contract was if West held the $\diamond$K as the entry for his hearts. However, it was crucial that West's $\diamond$K be preserved for later.

After winning the $\heartsuit$K, declarer led the $\diamond$Q at trick two. East was ready. He jumped up with his $\diamond$A and returned his last heart. Declarer was now helpless. He had to continue to develop dummy's diamond suit. Alas, West won the $\diamond$K and cashed four heart tricks. Down two.

If East had played "second hand low" when the $\diamond$Q was led, West's $\diamond$K would have been forced out. When East got in later with his $\diamond$A, he would be "heartless," and unable to reach West's four winning heart tricks.

By the way: If East held the $\diamond$K instead of the $\diamond$A, it would have been just as important for him to play "second hand high." Now, that would be defense with a capital "D."

If dummy has a singleton in a suit contract, any signal by third hand is suit preference.

North (dummy)

Contract: 4♠
Lead: ◇ A

♠ 9 5 4 2
♡ A Q J 5
◇ Q
♣ A K J 9

West (you)
♠ A Q 3
♡ 9
◇ A K J 8 4
♣ 8 6 5 4

West	North	East	South
1◇	Dbl	Pass	2♠
Pass	4♠	All Pass	

You lead the ◇ A with a hand that offers definite prospects of defeating their game. Partner follows with the ◇ 2 and declarer plays the ◇ 5. You're delighted that dummy lacks the ♠ K, but you're disappointed (although not surprised) to see the singleton diamond. Before reading on, what would you lead at trick two?

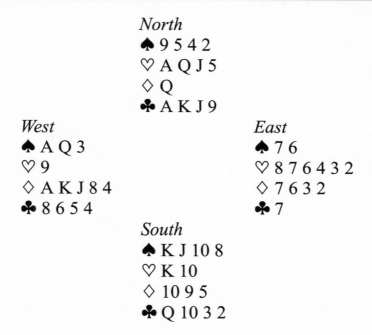

North
♠ 9 5 4 2
♡ A Q J 5
◇ Q
♣ A K J 9

West
♠ A Q 3
♡ 9
◇ A K J 8 4
♣ 8 6 5 4

East
♠ 7 6
♡ 8 7 6 4 3 2
◇ 7 6 3 2
♣ 7

South
♠ K J 10 8
♡ K 10
◇ 10 9 5
♣ Q 10 3 2

Did you lead your ♡9, hoping that partner had the ♡K or that you'd get a ruff? No way! South needs the ♡K for his jump, and is going to draw trump ASAP.

Let's examine the evidence. Partner's ◇2 says that he likes clubs. You should shift to the ♣4.

Declarer will win your club shift in dummy and finesse trumps. You win, and lead a second club. Partner ruffs, and your ♠A is the setting trick. Well done!

Cover an honor with an honor only when: you have a realistic chance to promote something for yourself or your partner.

This definitely is a lot to remember and understand. Most players are content to walk around chanting: "Cover an honor with an honor."

However, while the latter statement is short and easy to remember, it is not very accurate. For example:

You are East, defending a 4♠ contract after South's weak 2♠ bid was raised to game. Here are the trumps for you and dummy:

North (dummy)
♠ Q 5 4 2

East (you)
♠ K 3

Declarer wins partner's opening lead on the board and leads the ♠Q. Are you tempted to cover?

156

In this case, covering would be ridiculous, and when the ♠Q is led, you must duck smoothly. How can you know this?

The "secret" is counting. Declarer started with six spades. Dummy has four, while you have two. Once you subtract from 13, you know that partner started with one spade. Regardless of what singleton he has, there is no way to promote something for him. Obviously, you can't promote anything for yourself. Therefore, do not "cover an honor with an honor."

By smoothly playing low, you give declarer no clue that you have the king. This could pay huge dividends; after all, declarer might go up with his ace. Many players mistakenly believe that with 10 cards missing the king, they should play for the drop.

By the way: Just in case declarer chose to open 2♠ with ♠ J 10 9 8 7 6, playing low avoids everyone's worst bridge nightmare — playing your trump king on the same trick as your partner's trump ace.

A LEAD TO AVOID

Even in notrump, avoid an opening lead from a four-card suit with the ace (but no king).

All of us were taught not to lead away from an ace on opening lead against a suit contract. Experience suggests that this advice also applies to notrump. With this combination of cards, you're more likely to give away a trick than you are to *develop* additional tricks.

What would you lead against 1NT – 3NT?

♠ 9 8 7 ♡ 6 4 2 ◇ A J 6 3 ♣ Q 6 2
Lead the ♠9, top-of-nothing.

♠ K 7 5 3 ♡ A 7 5 3 ◇ 9 6 4 ♣ 6 2
Lead the ♠3. Prefer to try to establish "aceless" suits.

♠ Q 4 ♡ A 9 7 4 2 ◇ J 9 ♣ 10 5 4 3
Lead the ♡4. With a five-card suit, you have better chances of developing a lot of tricks, and are less likely to give something away.

Logical exception: It's okay to lead from the ace when partner promised length in that suit.

Complete List
of
Tip Summaries

Chapter 1 - Starting Off Right

Page #

13. Bidding can be defined as an exchange of relevant information. You don't have to talk about every suit in your hand.

14. When your partner thinks for a long time and then passes, you are NOT barred.

16. Bidding from hand records is a great way to fine-tune the partnership, and it's fun.

18. When partner's bid leads to a bad result, don't assume he made a mistake — it could just be the "luck of the cards."

20. The right time to wheel out a convention is NOT in the middle of the auction.

Chapter 2 - Hand Evaluation

Chapter 3 - Opener

Chapter 4 - Responder

Chapter 5 - Notrump

Chapter 6 - Slam

Page #

75. After a limit raise, opener should not consider slam without a singleton or void.

76. When responder wants to make a forcing raise in opener's major, Jacoby 2NT is an excellent convention to explore for slam.

78. If partner opens 2♣, respond 2♢ unless you have a long, strong suit.

80. If partner invites a notrump slam with a jump to 4NT, you're welcome to bid a suit.

82. A "slam try" cue-bid promises first OR second-round control in that suit.

Chapter 7 - Preempts

Chapter 8 - Cue-Bids

Chapter 9 - Overcalls

Page #

111. A jump-overcall in the balancing seat shows a good hand. It is not a Weak Jump Overcall (WJO).

112. If you have a good hand, it's okay to overcall at the one level with a lousy five-card suit.

113. An overcall at the 2+ level usually includes VOB. However, never say never.

114. The higher the level of RHO's initial action, the better your hand must be in order to bid or double.

116. If you'd like to bid after an opponent's three-level preempt, think 3NT.

118. You don't need a stopper in opener's suit to balance with 1NT.

120. After partner overcalls at the one level, a new suit should not be forcing.

Chapter 10 - Doubles

Chapter 11 - Declarer

Chapter 12 - Defense

Glossary
&
Recommended
Reading

1NT Response to Major — Refers to the standard treatment (6-10 HCP) as well as 1NT Forcing.

2/1 Auctions — References in this book apply to both the traditional 10+ HCP as well as the two-over-one game-forcing style.

2♣ Opening — A strong, artificial, and forcing opening bid used with powerhouse hands when playing weak two-bids. Opener has either a long suit or a balanced hand too strong to open 2NT.

4-3-3-3 — This distribution, where the four-card suit is not specified.

5-5 — At least five cards in each of two suits.

Alertable — In duplicate bridge, some artificial calls made by a player must be "alerted" by his partner to inform the opponents that the action was not natural.

Artificial Bid — A bid that does not promise the suit that was named.

Balanced Distribution — A hand with no singleton or void, and at most one doubleton. Balanced patterns are: 4-4-3-2, 4-3-3-3 and 5-3-3-2.

Balancing Seat — A player is said to be in the balancing seat when his pass would end the auction. One should often try to reopen rather than allow the opponents to play in a low-level contract.

Bid — 1♣ through 7NT. Does not include pass, double, or redouble.

"The Board" — Refers to dummy.

Call — Any bid, pass, double, or redouble.

Cold — Slang for a contract that is sure to make.

"Colors" — Vulnerability. In duplicate, red stands for vulnerable, white for nonvulnerable.

Control (noun) — A holding that prevents the opponents from winning the first two tricks in a suit.

Count, as in "18 count" — 18 HCP.

Cue-Bid — An artificial, forcing bid in the opponent's suit. Also, a bid of a new suit after the trump suit has been established (as a slam try).

Dbl — Double.

Distribution — The number of cards in each suit.

Distribution Points — The total of a player's HCP and his "short-suit" points after a fit is found.

Draw(ing) Trumps — Leading trumps, to remove as many as possible from the opponents' hands.

Duck — To play a small card, surrendering a trick you might have won.

Entry — A holding that provides access to a hand. Efficient use of entries is crucial for both sides.

Favorable Vulnerability — You are not vulnerable, the opponents are.

Fit — A term referring to the partnership's combined assets with respect to a suit, usually trump.

HCP — High-card points.

Intermediates — Middle cards such as the 10, 9, 8.

Jacoby 2NT — Artificial, forcing raise of opener's major. Opener shows a singleton if he has one.

Jacoby Transfer — Used in response to notrump opening bids, or a natural notrump overcall. A diamond response promises heart length, while a heart bid shows at least five spades. Opener must bid the suit responder has "shown."

Law of Total Tricks ("The LAW") — You are always safe bidding to the level equal to your side's number of trumps. It is extremely helpful when judging whether or not to bid on in competitive auctions. It is based on the concept that "Trump Length is Everything."

LHO — Left-hand opponent.

Limit Raise — Responder's invitational raise from one to three of a suit, promising 10-12 distribution points and trump support.

Michaels Cue-Bid — An overcall in the opponent's suit that shows at least five cards in each of two suits. The emphasis is on the unbid major(s).

Natural — A bid which promises the suit named.

New Minor Forcing — After opener's rebid of 1NT or 2NT, responder's bid in an unbid minor asks opener about his major-suit length. Responder usually has a five-card major with at least game-invitational values.

Open — Make the first bid.

Preempt — A jump bid based on a long suit and a weak hand. The intention is to deprive the opponents of bidding space and make it harder for them to communicate and reach their optimal contract.

Quick Trick — A high-card holding that will usually result in a trick (also known as defensive tricks).
    AK = 2   AQ = 1 ½   A = 1   KQ = 1   Kx = ½

Reverse — Opener's rebid at the two level in a suit that is higher-ranking than his first bid. It shows at least 17 points and promises five or six cards in his first suit. This topic causes more anxiety than any other.

RHO — Right-hand opponent.

The Rule of 20 — Used to evaluate whether or not to open borderline hands in first and second seat. Add the length of your two longest suits to your HCP. With 20 or more, open the bidding in a suit at the one level.

Shape — See "Distribution."

Side Suit(s) — Any suit other than trumps.

Signoff — A bid intended to end the auction. Sometimes referred to as a *drop-dead bid*.

Splinter Bid — A convention featuring a jump into a short suit (void or singleton), promising good support for partner and values for game or slam.

Stopper — A card or combination of cards that prevents the opponents from running a suit in a notrump contract.

Tenace — A combination of non-consecutive honors. Some examples are KJ and AQ.

Unfavorable Vulnerability — You are vulnerable, the opponents are not.

Unusual Notrump Overcall — A method of showing length in the two lower unbid suits after an opponent opens the bidding.

VOB — Stands for: Enough **V**alues to **O**pen the **B**idding, but not much more.

xx — Small cards; in this case, exactly two.

Yarborough — A hand with no card above a nine.

HIGHLY RECOMMENDED

Hardcover Books by Marty Bergen

MARTY SEZ	$17.95
MARTY SEZ - VOLUME 2	$17.95
POINTS SCHMOINTS!	$19.95
More POINTS SCHMOINTS!	$19.95
Schlemiel...Schlimazel? Mensch	$14.95

(not a bridge book)

·· UNPRECEDENTED OFFER ··

If your purchase of Marty's hardcover books exceeds $25, you will automatically receive a 50% discount. Personalized autographs available upon request.

Softcover Books by Marty Bergen

1NT Forcing		$5.95
Evaluate Your Hand Like an Expert		$5.95
Introduction to Negative Doubles		$6.95
Negative Doubles		$9.95
Better Bidding With Bergen 1 –		
Uncontested Auctions		$11.95
Better Bidding With Bergen 2 –		
Competitive Bidding		$11.95
Marty's Reference book		
on Conventions	~~$9.95~~	$7.00

NOW AVAILABLE

CDs by Marty Bergen

POINTS SCHMOINTS! ~~$29.95~~ $25
New interactive version of the award-winning book.

Marty Sez... ~~$24.95~~ $20
114 of Bergen's best bridge secrets.

· · FREE SHIPPING ON ALL SOFTWARE · ·
(in the U.S.)

Software by Mike Lawrence

Counting at Bridge ~~$34.95~~ $30
Shows you ways to gather and use information.

Private Bridge Lessons, Vol. 1 ~~$34.95~~ $30
Declarer techniques that everybody needs to know.

Private Bridge Lessons, Vol. 2 ~~$34.95~~ $30
Over 100 hands with interactive feedback.

Defense ~~$34.95~~ $30
Avoid errors and take as many tricks as possible.

Two Over One ~~$34.95~~ $30
Many hands to maximize your game and slam bidding.

Conventions ~~$60.00~~ $48
A must for every partnership.

Now Available

CDs By Larry Cohen

Play Bridge With Larry Cohen
An exciting opportunity to play question-and-answer
with a 17-time national champion. "One of the best
products to come along in years. Easy-to-use. Suitable
for every player who wishes to improve his scores."

Day 1	~~$29.95~~	$26
Day 2	~~$29.95~~	$26
Day 3	~~$29.95~~	$26

Software By Fred Gitelman

Bridge Master 2000   ~~$59.95~~ $48
"Best software ever created for improving your
declarer play."

Books by Eddie Kantar

A Treasury of Bridge Bidding Tips	$11.95
Take Your Tricks (Declarer Play)	$12.95
Defensive Tips for Bad Card Holders	$12.95

Unique Gift Suggestion!
*365 Bridge Hands
with Expert Analysis*   ~~$13.95~~ $5

ONE-ON-ONE WITH MARTY

Why not improve your bridge with an experienced, knowledgeable teacher? Enjoy a private bridge lesson with Marty Bergen. You choose the format and topics, including Q&A, conventions, bidding, and cardplay.

Marty is available for lessons via phone and e-mail. Beginners, intermediates, and advanced players will all benefit from his clear and helpful teaching style.

For further information, please call the number below, or e-mail Marty at: mbergen@mindspring.com

ORDERING INFORMATION

To place your order, call Marty toll-free at
1-800-386-7432
all credit cards are welcome

Or send a check or money order (U.S. currency), to:

Marty Bergen
9 River Chase Terrace
Palm Beach Gardens, FL 33418-6817

Please include $3 postage and handling for each order.

Postage is FREE if your order includes
any of Marty's hardcover books.